SHOP
AROUND

SHOP AROUND

Growing Up With Motown In a Sinatra Household

by **Bruce Jenkins**

Printed in the United States of America

FIRST EDITION
ISBN 978-0986189814

Wellstone Books
an imprint of the Wellstone Center in the Redwoods
858 Amigo Road
Soquel, CA 95073

Distributed by Publishers Group West

Contents

Piano recital at the home of Nat King Cole, 1960.
It almost went well.

Chapter 1

Don't Mind Me

I t was not a beaten path. I'm fairly certain of that, unless there were any other white kids venturing into a black-women's hair salon. The crazy part is that I actually had some business there.

It was the fall of 1965, my junior year at Santa Monica High School, and I was hooked on soul music. I could hang with the Beatles, the Stones and the Beach Boys if necessary, but my radio dial was set to KGFJ and KDAY, a couple of Southern California stations devoted to Motown, Stax and the more esoteric R&B labels of the day.

You could find the best of Marvin Gaye, the Supremes and the Temptations at any record store. It wasn't so easy tracking down Jimmy Reed, Bo Diddley or the Sapphires. That would mean a trip into the heart of Watts or East L.A, not a terribly good idea in the mid-'60s, and I'd only been driving a few months. The beach town of Santa Monica, as it turned out, was an excellent place to grasp the meaning of civil rights and broaden one's cultural horizons.

I'm not sure how I found out about that hair salon, but I suspect the information came from Jake Whidbee, my best friend at the time. We'd met in the eighth grade, writing sports stories for the *Lincoln Railsplitter*, our junior-high school newspaper, and I bonded almost instantly with Jake, an African-American kid with a brilliant mind and crackling sense of humor.

On the surface, we couldn't have been more different. I was raised in Malibu, the son of a musician (Gordon Jenkins) who had the wisdom to move there in 1945. Jake was from Compton but lived with his grandmother on the predominantly black south side of Santa Monica. Yet we connected on every level. We spent the night at each other's houses, marveled at Jim Murray's exquisite columns in the *L.A. Times*, and watched the likes of Jerry West, Elgin Baylor, Sandy Koufax and Don Drysdale perform in person.

As I look back, that was the beauty of Santa Monica in those days. I rode the bus twenty-five miles from Malibu (where only grade schools existed) every day for six years, digesting the rewards of a true melting pot: blacks, Jews, Asians and Mexicans all well represented in my classes and sports teams. Moving on to Cal-Berkeley a little later was hardly a culture shock for me in that regard, merely an extension of my teenage experience.

What I couldn't have expected, under any circumstances, was the miracle of that hair salon, maybe a mile's walk from campus. In a little back room, past the stylists and the implements of their trade, was a rack full of 45s for sale. These were two-sided vinyl recordings, with the hit song on one side and a "B" take on the other. The distribution of music is infinitely more sophisticated these days, but back then, it was all about *records*: those precious 45s or full-sized 33 $\frac{1}{3}$-rpm albums.

I'm certain many weeks would pass without any sign of white folks in that room. The 45s were there for the pleasure of customers, a dandy little secret on the southwestern edge of town. I struggled to explain my presence the first time in, but it couldn't have been a big puzzle. I'd heard about the records. On subsequent visits, I could tell the ladies got a big kick out of this skinny kid in his tidy gray sweater, so very far from home, and they couldn't have been nicer, telling me, "Go on back, find what you like." Walking out of there, with my excellent new stash of Eddie Holman, the Autographs, Koko Taylor and Alvin Cash & the Crawlers, I'd be thrilled to the core.

I was always hoping for a fresh discovery to shake me up like the record that, several years before, had changed my life. In the third week of October 1960, Smokey Robinson and the Miracles released two minutes and fifty seconds of pulsating excitement called "Shop Around." Rhythm-and-blues artists had been around for decades, and I knew all about the pioneering Ray Charles, already a fixture on the scene, but this was different. This was the man, Smokey, whose clever lyrics would form Motown's foundation, and like all the great ones — Bobby Bland, Otis Redding, Jackie Wilson — nobody ever sang like Smokey. He had a way of turning single syllables (like the word "yeah") into rapid-fire, five-note virtuosity, an absolute master of style and technique. It's never easy ranking your favorites, but I know that no single record knocked me out — like, flat on the ground — like "Shop Around." Just because it was so entirely fresh, in my mind the signal of a brand-new day. I was twelve years old, radio at the bedside, just waiting for Smokey to come back.

That bedroom was my musical sanctuary, a veritable secret within my own home. I was the child of two formidable musicians: Beverly, a top-notch solo vocalist on national radio throughout the 1940s, and Gordon, whose accomplishments ran fully off the charts. Composer, arranger, conductor, performer — he did everything but kick the field goals. He was inducted into the Songwriters Hall of Fame, arranged and conducted eight albums with Frank Sinatra, discovered the Weavers, worked extensively with Louis Armstrong, Judy Garland and Nat Cole. Sinatra revered my father's work, and I say that with assurance, having interviewed him at his Beverly Hills home in 1990. Sinatra told me he had more respect for my father's command of an orchestra than anyone else he worked with, and I watched him brought to tears as the memories came to life. I'd often heard the word "genius" associated with Gordon's name, and I came to believe that recklessly misused word truly applied in his case.

We're all influenced so heavily by our musical upbringing, and my parents had a passionate and comprehensive understanding that covered the spectrum: jazz, blues, big-band, gospel, Dixieland, symphonies, the opera. Early on, Gor (as I called him) built a studio separate from the house, so as not to be bothered by adolescent noise. My bedroom was downstairs and I could see that studio, not thirty feet away, out my window. Thirty feet and thousands of musical miles.

Each morning at dawn he'd sit down at his magnificent Steinway piano and crank out the scales, up and down, shifting keys, always in strict routine. For him that was batting practice, building rhythm in his hands and precise musical structure in his head. If a deadline loomed, he'd then begin arranging: right hand on the keyboard, left hand scribbling notes on a score sheet with a long-trusted fountain pen. They said he worked with astounding speed, able to arrange an entire album for Sinatra and a forty-piece orchestra in a matter of days, if necessary. Amazingly, he always seemed to be done working around noon, at which point he'd set off for the Las Posas Country Club in Camarillo, thirty miles to the north, and a round of golf. People reveled in his celebrity up there, although there was scant little evidence; Gor tended to play with a group of airline pilots, superbly capable, self-effacing guys with a roaring sense of humor. That was always his taste in companions: rarely someone as conspicuous as Sinatra, Garland or Jonathan Winters (my eternal god of comedy; I almost passed out when he showed up at the house one day). Rather, with the cocktails flowing, our living room was graced by lifelong musicians, always the best guys in town, but just as importantly, hardy drinkers who didn't take themselves too seriously.

Gracious, what a setup he had. Self-taught on at least a dozen instruments, he was never caught short: piano, organ, drums, vibraphone, electric and bass guitars, the banjo. None of which I could play worth a damn. I always felt that I *understood* music with the best of them, but I froze at the notion of performing, and besides, what was the point? My mother was one of the best sight-readers in all of Los Angeles, able to sing anything in any key, and my father was Gordon Jenkins. Who the hell am I, the sixth guy in the Dave Clark Five? I wasn't going to come close to their virtuosity, ever, no chance. And so I arrived at the moment of clarity: a piano recital at the Beverly Hills home of Nat and Maria Cole in 1960. The room was filled with youthful brilliance, including little Natalie (she and her sister were called "Cookie" and "Sweetie" in those days). And there I was, a promising look in my dandy black suit, but fooling no one when the lights came on. I was eleven, anxious to just throw up my hands and play Little League, and that would be the path. (Couldn't hit the curveball, but that's another mournful tale.)

My father had moved to Malibu from Hollywood to escape all the excessive blathering bullshit, and in doing so, he created an authentic recording studio right there at home. He had one of the first 8-track mixing boards produced by the 3M company, later advancing to a 16-track machine of the highest order. He always had the best of everything: Sennheiser microphones, Ampex reel-to-reel tape recorder, Fender bass, Musser vibes. One day I saw my mother and two of my dad's favorite horn players out there, laying down tracks. She turned four takes into four-part harmony while the horns did their thing and my dad filled in the guitar, bass and drum parts, adding what sounded like a string section through the magic of his multifaceted Thomas organ. With the subtle touches of a master engineer, he turned four people into a full-blown orchestra and chorus. I loved watching them laugh so heartily while hearing the playback, a priceless memory, for so often in my house, laughter wasn't about a funny joke. It was the natural reaction to a really kick-ass piece of music. Just cracked 'em up every time, depending on the mood. And sometimes the tears would flow, out of sheer appreciation.

This is why "Shop Around," and the wondrous torrent of soul music that followed, saved my life. To be brutally honest, Gor had no use for R&B or just about anything that hit the pop-station airwaves after 1955. He was repulsed to the point of illness by Elvis Presley and the Beatles, and while quite often I could see his point, I figured he'd offer at least a *glimmer* of appreciation for Steely Dan or Tower of Power. If so, he never let on. To break through his wall, you'd better be Stan Getz, Wes Montgomery or Jack Jones, someone he connected to that old-style professionalism, and that's simply how it was. I had my own tape recorder alongside the bed, religiously taping L.A. stations with hopes of my favorite songs coming on, but I had to be very careful about the volume.

My mother was a bit more sympathetic. I can recall times, in my early thirties, when she'd plug into my fondness for Stevie Wonder, James Brown and especially Aretha Franklin. She'd grown up hearing the greatest blues and gospel artists belting out the down-home truth, and Aretha's range and compassion particularly hit home with her. I spun out the usual assortment of favorites — "Respect," "Natural Woman," "Think," "Chain of Fools" — but she was especially fond of "Drown in My Own Tears" and Aretha's accompanying piano. "That's a little girl that grew up in church," she told me. (Good call: Aretha was a preacher's daughter and traveled around with her father on gospel-performance tours.) "Nothin' fancy about that piano, but if that's not the real thing, I'll put in with ya." So, absolutely, Beverly *got* all that, and here's where the story turns. In researching the lives of my parents for a biography I wrote called *Goodbye: In Search of Gordon Jenkins* after my father's death in 1984, I was delighted to discover that we had a tremendous amount of musical experience in common. In a sense, lying beside my radio with the volume at a reasonable level, I was living their lives all over again.

Gordon and Beverly, mid-70s.
Days of wine and roses in Malibu.

Chapter 2

Mother Sang the Blues

Beverly was the daughter of an Oklahoma oilman, raised in a stately mansion and a world of opulence. She didn't quite take to that, or the stuffy music she was hearing during her teens in the 1920s. Her family had a black maid, by the name of Pauline, who grew quite fond of Beverly. One day Pauline invited the girl into her private quarters and started spinning records, the raw, down-deep blues numbers of the day. "Race records," as they were called in the music business, and they were *exactly* what my mother wanted to hear.

"I used to go sit outside the Holy Roller churches when these hotshot girls — and I mean, the real flashers — would come in from Kansas City," she once told me. "They could dance and sing the blues better than anybody. And see, Pauline came from Kansas City and she got me wise to everything. I used to slide over there to see what was goin' on. She knew about Bennie Moten and Bessie Smith, everybody. We only had one place to buy records in the town of Bristow, and that was Stone's Hardware. I didn't go there. Pauline had everything I needed to know about."

That little room became Beverly's haven, and the genesis of all to come. She and her sister moved boldly to New York in their early twenties, determined to sing their way into prominence, and they did precisely that. They mastered every assignment that came their way, but for Beverly, with Pauline's precious 78s locked safely in mind, blues was the thing. She hadn't come from despair, wicked segregation or the hopelessness of the cotton fields, nor would she even pretend to be in the class of Mildred Bailey or Billie Holiday. But she connected most deeply with that world. The music was in her soul, and whenever a blues number came her way, particularly in those glorious radio days, she was *ready*. In the words of the late Dick Eckels, one of my dad's top trumpet players, "as ready as a drunk in the Hi-Ho Motel."

My father knew all about Beverly in the early '40s, when they were both working radio shows in Los Angeles. She had become a soloist, with a voice so distinctive, she even stood out in a chorus. When I interviewed Frank Sinatra for my father's biography, I mentioned her singing style and his eyes lit up: "Oooh, yeah. What a sound. What a sound! You'd have four hundred singers around town and one voice would come out like that."

She was lookin' pretty good, too. My dad was married at the time, but that never stopped him from developing heavy crushes on a number of singers, often following through right into the bedroom. His wife, Nan, was a fine and sturdy woman who raised three children, but she had no feel for good music. There's nothing more costly to a marriage than complete disinterest in your partner's passion, and I once heard Gor tell a friend that when he'd come home from a live radio gig, stoked out of his mind, Nan not only shrugged it off, she hadn't even listened to the show. That can wear on someone after a while. Grounds for a randy tour through the world of comely female singers? Not in the eyes of your local pastor — but this was Hollywood, where the sudden convergence of talent so often leads scandalously to romance. There wasn't a more scrupulous musician in town when it came to arrangements and the finite precision of an orchestra, but in terms of living up to a marriage vow, Gor had no scruples whatsoever.

Shift now to the greatest national celebration in the history of the United States, that rarest of events in which the whole damned country felt surges of ecstasy and relief. The end of World War II launched weeks of revelry in 1945, and it was in that setting that Gordon and Beverly met at a Hollywood party. He was musical director of the *Auto-Lite* show on radio, featuring singer Dick Haymes and broadcast nationally. Haymes was among the most admired talents of his time, a handsome, athletic fellow who replaced Sinatra as Tommy Dorsey's lead singer in 1942. He drew constant comparisons to Sinatra, some preferring his friendly, middle-America charm to Sinatra's uptown edge. Later in life, Haymes was besieged by debt, a failed movie career and a serious drinking problem, but he was in his absolute prime with my father in one of the most ambitious under-takings in radio history.

The show launched on NBC in June 1944, switched to CBS in 1945, and gained widespread attention. Marveling at the fact that Jenkins had assembled sixty-five people on stage, including a thirty-one-piece orchestra and twenty singers, the *Milwaukee Journal* noted that "Haymes acts as if he were in the midst of a cozy gathering. His studio audiences do not. The crowds of servicemen, the young and the old who surge into Studio A at CBS in Hollywood, are visibly impressed by the size of the cast. Only in a lavish Broadway production — an 'Oklahoma,' for example — are there as many performers filling the stage."

The cast also included Cliff Arquette, a wonderful humorist (and grandfather to Rosanna, Patricia and David Arquette) who later became known for his improvisational wit on *The Hollywood Squares*. Such notables as Judy Garland, Nat Cole, Betty Grable, Lana Turner, Dorothy Lamour and Peggy Lee made appearances. And in the beginning, it was all about the war effort. Auto-Lite produced sparkplugs, batteries and other electrical products, and the show had cheery, enthusiastic ads about the Auto-Lite-powered Mustang fighters bombing overseas targets. An old Jenkins scrapbook reveals two letters of commendation from the Treasury Department, citing my father's contributions to the cause, and *Radio Life* magazine honored him as the nation's most popular arranger-conductor in 1944 and '45.

The half-hour show ran for thirty-nine consecutive weeks each year, through the summer of '48, and Gor's lightning-speed work pace was never more valuable. He and Tom Adair, a noted songwriter who penned a number of hits, came up with jaunty "mini-operas" each week, built around themes, clever dialogue and original music. At war's end, he happened to be looking for a "girl singer," as they were known at the time, to blend in with four guys. They became "Four Hits and a Miss," featuring Beverly's lead vocals, and as the sparks of romance flew, a torrid love affair began.

What a dreamy setting for their special gifts: two live shows every night — one for the East Coast, then one for the West — in an absolute perform-or-bust setting. There were no retakes, no chance to cover for a mistake, and the two of them couldn't have been happier. They were born to do their flat-out best work *right now*, no jimmy-jackin' around. Between shows, most everyone would head to a couple of local taverns across from the studio's Vine Street entrance. I never once saw my mother get sloppy or even out of character in any setting, so I doubt if she took more than a couple of sips. Gor was up for a stiff one, definitely. And some of the band guys took the mission quite seriously, lurching back for the West Coast show in a whole new mood. "Some of those late shows were … interesting, shall we say," one of the band members' wives told me. "But never a bust. Always professional. Hell, Gordy loved guys who were real good drinkers and played great."

I'm not sure one could pinpoint the highlight of my mother's career. Way back in 1936, she was a standout in the chorus behind the great Kay Thompson, one of the most gifted all-around entertainers in the history of show business, on the CBS *Chesterfield Hour.* That episode launched Beverly's career and she never looked back. But her work on the *Manhattan Tower* album, right at the beginning of her relationship with Gordon, was deeply inspired. One song in particular, "Married I Can Always Get," really showcased her virtuosity. It's a chart demanding great range, extremely difficult to sing well, and I've always thought the lyrics ranked with my father's finest. In part:

It's not for me
With all its smug connubial joys
That ever-constant smashing of toys
Wrecks your poise
While hubby is out with the boys

No wedding gown
For this silhouette
Married I can always get

I'll live the life that I'm used to
I'll get a ring when I choose to
Because by now I have found
That the nicest rings are on a merry-go-'round

I'll be blase
With any man whose motives are base
I'll keep each wily wolf in his place
'Til the chase finally ends in embrace
But as for wedlock, unlock me, my pet
Married I can always get

I'll go the way that the wind blows
Along the path that is primrose
I have my plan all rehearsed

I will kiss anybody who will kiss me first

I'll take a cruise
Into a more adventurous clime
And if the captain's still in his prime
He will find
You don't have to sail all the time

I want to stick to romantic roulette
Married I can always get

My parents made it official in 1946, dashing off to Juarez, Mexico, for a quickie wedding (she was also married at the time, quite unhappily). They'd wait until later to sort out their divorces and all that jazz. They looked upon each other with a sense of destiny, that it was *far* more than a fling. Whether my dad went astray at times over the years, I'll never be sure; I never saw or heard anything to that effect. I do know that they were wildly in love until my father's death in 1984, and I'd been that very lucky kid who never heard his parents raise their voices to each other.

By the time I was out on my own, attending UC Berkeley in the fall of '66 and then hooking up with the *San Francisco Chronicle* in 1973, I gravitated naturally toward musicians. I roomed with a Marin County-raised drummer named Scott Murphy for three years at Cal and we were later housemates in Corte Madera. I remember the joy in my mother's face when Scott and the guys in his various bands came down to Malibu for a visit. She was thrilled that I plugged into that world, even from a distance. Living in Marin (1974–1984) gave me a chance to see Huey Lewis in his early days, with a band called Clover, and here was a true kindred spirit, someone who had grown up as a soul-music enthusiast and had it coursing through his veins. I got to know Huey before he ruled the world and found it immensely satisfying that a man of his exquisite taste could reach the heights of celebrity.

The connection my mother found most interesting, though, was with Tower of Power. Their first album (*East Bay Grease*) carried me right through my senior year at Cal. I play their stuff religiously to this day, and even though I've long since memorized every arrangement, every nuance, it still speaks to innovation and ingenuity. Murphy had an audition with Tower at a time their phenomenal drummer, Dave Garibaldi, had left the band, and although he didn't get the gig, Scott got to know some of the guys. I got to meet the great Emilio Castillo, the saxophonist/lead singer who had grown up in Detroit, the heart of Motown, and embraced that music with fervent devotion. I learned that baritone sax player Steve "Doc" Kupka was a huge fan of my father's music, and the two of us have been friends for forty-odd years. When I temporarily moved back into the Malibu house in the late 1980s (trying to make a relationship work), Doc was living in L.A. and made many nocturnal visits, arriving right around my mother's bedtime, chatting for a while and then going furiously to work, scribbling lyrics and musical notations into an 8x10 notepad until the morning hours. Doc found it so comforting to be in the house of Gordon Jenkins, even though he'd passed away, keeping the tradition of great songwriting alive.

So, while we're on the subject, how about a little contrast. To say the least, Gor and Doc came from entirely different worlds (condensed for brevity):

Beautiful girls
Walk a little slower when you walk by me
Lingering sunsets

Stay a little longer with the lonely sea
Children everywhere
When you shoot at bad men, shoot at me
Take me to that strange enchanted land
Grown-ups seldom understand
Wandering rainbows
Leave a bit of color for my heart to own
Stars in the sky
Make my wish come true before the night has
flown
And let the music play
As long as there's a song to sing
And I will stay younger than spring

— Jenkins' "This Is All I Ask," 1956

There is only so much oil in the ground
Sooner or later, there won't be none around
Tell that to your children
While you're drivin' round downtown
That there's only so much oil in the ground

'Cause there's only so much oil in the earth
Sooner or later, gonna be a heavy-duty dearth

And there won't be too much time
For no merriment or mirth
'Cause there's only so much oil in the earth

There's no excuse
For our abuse
Can't cut loose
Without that juice

— Kupka/Castillo's "Only So Much Oil," 1973

Gor never had much use for Tower, and lord knows, I tried to convince him. It wasn't that he doubted the musicianship; it's impossible to hear Garibaldi, bassist Rocco Prestia or Greg Adams' horn arrangements and not realize something exceptional is going on. It just wasn't what he wanted to hear. He was intensely rigid that way. It was as if he closed the door on his musical exploration around the mid-'50s and never reopened it. I'm sure it was Presley who triggered his theories of musical Armageddon, but even the classier stuff left him rather cold. Beverly wasn't at all that way. She loved that I knew Doc Kupka and she'd linger in the room if I had some Tower on. It was always that way, going back to my mid-teens and the little tape recorder in my bedroom. Maybe it wasn't exactly her thing, but she loved that rhythm-and-blues was at the core of my musical taste, and that's a bond that can never be broken.

One thing that disgusted the three of us, unconditionally: With the arrival of rock 'n' roll and later the evolution into punk rock and heavy metal, a band member's *looks* became critical. Never mind if he couldn't play a complex chord to save his life. Up there on stage, man, with his shirt off, grabbing his crotch and leaping about, he was *killing*. Chicks going *berserk*. There's nothing like the thrill of a live show, going back to Benny Goodman's swingin' years and all that came before, but don't you need a little musicianship along the way? If all you've got going is a radical hairstyle or a sexy body, isn't that cheating, somehow?

None of that nonsense was in play during the prime of my mother's career. I know she was particularly proud of her work on *Seven Dreams*, a fifty-one-minute concept album my father created in 1954. The piece followed a man's path through a number of fanciful endeavors, not all of them pleasant, each episode ending with the ringing of an alarm clock and the awakening from a dream. "Crescent City Blues," a Jenkins original, was the album's most compelling song and, thanks to Johnny Cash, a source of great controversy some months after its release.

It begins with the narrator on a train, destination unknown. Worn down by the banalities of life, he's in dire need of some truth. At one particular stop, "I stepped off for a breath of middle-western air," he says. "As I lit a cigarette, I heard a voice from a shack across the way."

It was the voice of Beverly Mahr, her married name and one she kept professionally for years. This was her blues voice at its finest, and it seems clear that Cash was enraptured. Why, he loved that song so much, he stole it outright and turned it into "Folsom Prison Blues." That's correct: Without Gor's "Crescent City Blues," Cash's famous prison tune never exists.

Talk about shameless thievery. My dad's complete lyrics are on the left, with crucial Cash passages on the right:

I hear the train
a-comin

It's rollin' round
the bend

And I ain't been
kissed, lord

Since I don't
know when

The boys in
Crescent City

Don't seem to know
I'm here

That lonesome whistle
seems to tell me

Oooh-oooh, Sue,
disappear

When I was just
a baby

My mama told me, Sue

I hear the train
a-comin'

It's rollin' round
the bend

And I ain't seen the
sunshine

Since I don't
know when

When I was just
a baby

My mama told me, Son

When you're grown up

*I want that you should
go and see and do*

*But I'm stuck in
Crescent City*

*Just watchin' life mo-
sey by*

When I hear that whis- *tle blowin'*	*When I hear that whis-* *tle blowin'*
I hang my head *and cry*	*I hang my head* *and cry*
I see the rich *folks eatin'*	*I bet there's rich* *folks eatin'*
In that fancy dinin' car	*In a fancy dinin' car*

*They're probably
havin' pheasant
breast*

And eastern caviar

Now I ain't cryin' envy

And I ain't cryin' mean

It's just they get to
see things

That I've never seen

If I owned that lone-
some whistle

If that railroad train
was mine

I bet I'd find a man

A little farther down
the line

Far from Crescent City

Is where I'd like
to stay

And I'd let that lone-
some whistle

Blow my blues away.

Well, if they freed me
from this prison

If that railroad train
was mine

I bet I'd move it on

A little farther down
the line

Far from Folsom Prison

That's where I want
to stay

And I'd let that lone-
some whistle

Blow my blues away.

I mean, holy shit!

It's a good thing for Cash that my father was a kind-hearted soul. He didn't want to ruin the man's career, he just wanted a private settlement of some kind. At first, Cash's representatives thought the lawsuit was a joke — but they hadn't heard my dad's recording. When the evidence came forth, they piped down real quick. Completely behind the scenes, with no media attention, my father was awarded $175,000 — a fair amount of cash at the time, but a relative pittance considering the nature of the crime.

Cash, of course, went on to great fame and somehow survived this mess. Not that my mom much cared. She knew her version blew Cash's into the tumblin' tumbleweeds. She was about as diplomatic as they come, but I'll never forget her saying one time, around cocktail hour, "You know, I never thought that man could sing worth a damn."

ONE-A
ALCOHOL BLUES:SONNY BOY WILLIAMSON
EMPTY BED BLUES:BESSIE SMITH
YOU'RE NOT THE ONLY OYSTER:FATS WALLER
TAKE YOUR TOMORROW:FRANK TRUMBAUER
JUBILEE TIME:KAY THOMPSON,WM. BROS.
SINGING THE BLUES:BIX
ROCKIN' CHAIR:LOUIS ARMSTRONG
JACK-LOUIE BLUES:TGRDN AND LOUIS
BOX CAR BLUES:WINGY MANNONE

ONE-B
CROSS YOUR HEART:ARTIE SHAW
BILLIE'S BLUES:B. HOLLIDAY
SUMMIT RIDGE DRIVE:ARTIE SHAW
REAL GONE GUY:NELLIE LUTCHER
OUT OF NOWHERE:JAKE HAMMOND
WORLD ON A STRING:MILDRED BAILEY
HOT TOWN:FESS WILLIAMS
DING DONG BLUES:BENNY MOTEN
PASS OUT LIGHTLY: "   "

TWO-A
CHICKEN ALA KING:COUSIN JOE
RICH MAN IN GRAVEYARD:" "
I CAN'T GET STARTED:B. BERIGAN
LOCH LOMOND:MAXINE SULLIVAN
I'M COMIN',VIRGINIA: "   "
ONLY THE BEGINNING:HAROLD ARLEN
LETS FALL IN LOVE: "   "
YELLOW DOG BLUES:BESSIE SMITH
UNKNOWN BLUES:TAMPA RED
KIRKWOOD BLUES: "   "

TWO-B
WOLVERINE BLUES:BOB CROSBY
LOUISE,LOUISE: "   "
AT THE JAZZ BAND BALL: "
HAVE YOU EVER FELT THAT WAY?:MOTEN
GLAD WHEN YOU'RE DEAD:J. TEAGARDEN
MUGGLES: LOUIS ARMSTRONG
THINGS ABOUT COMIN' MY WAY:L.CARR
KNOCKIN' A JUG:L. ARMSTRONG
NO MATTER HOW SHE DOES IT:T RED
INDIAN CRADLE SONG:L. ARMSTRONG

THREE-A
AIN'T IT A SHAME?:WINGY MANNONE
WYNONNIE'S BLUES:W. HARRIS
SLEEPYTIME DOWN SOUTH:LOUIS
BLACK NAME BLUES:SONNY BOY W.
TROUBLE IN MIND:CHIPPIE HILL,LOUIS
GLAD WHEN YOU'RE DEAD:LOUIS
THINK YOU NEED A SHOT:JIMMIE GORDON
ST. JAMES INFIRMARY:LOUIS

THREE-B
HOW LONG,HOW LONG?:LEROY CARR
DALLAS BLUES:LOUIS
BASIN ST. BLUES:ELLA FITZGERALD
STARDUST:JIMMIE LUNCEFORD
RECKLESS MAN:TAMPA RED
CAN'T GET THAT STUFF NO MORE: TAMPA RED
ELMER'S TUNE:GLENN MILLER
BED BUG BLUES:BESSIE SMITH

FOUR-A
LAPLEGGED DRUNK AGAIN:LONNIE JOHNSON
DIANE:JACK TEAGARDEN
BLUE GHOST BLUES:LONNIE JOHNSON
MEMORIES OF YOU:LOUIS
YOU'RE LUCKY TO ME:LOUIS
IN A MIST:RED NORVO
ROCKIN' CHAIR:LOUIS ARMSTRONG
BASIN ST. BOOGIE:WILL BRADLEY
DON'T CALL ME BOY:BOB CROSBY

FOUR-B
MISSISSIPPI MUD:RHYTHM BOYS
ROLL 'EM PETE:JOE TURNER
GOIN' AWAY BLUES: "   "
MOSES SMOTE THE WATER:GOLDEN GATE QT.
ROYAL GARDEN BLUES: BIX
GOOSE PIMPLES: "
SENT FOR YOU YESTERDAY:BENNY GOODMAN
AND THE ANGELS SING: "   "
OOMPH FAH FAH: GOODMAN SEXTET
SLIPPED DISC: "   "

FIVE-A
FINE AND MELLOW:BILLIE HOLLIDAY
STRANGE FRUIT: "   "
BUTTER AND EGG MAN:VELMA M. AND LOUIS
CASEY JONES:BURL IVES AND BEVERLY
ST. LOUIS BLUES: LOUIS
ECHOES OF THE JUNGLE:DUKE ELLINGTON
LITTLE JOE:LOUIS
THEM THERE EYES:LOUIS
HURRY ON DOWN:NELLIE LUTCHER
BLUE SKIES:MEL POWELL

FIVE-B
STRIP POLKA:JOHNNY MERCER
SHOE SHINE RAG:JELLY ROLL MORTON
FRICTION:FESS WILLIAMS
C.C. AND ST. L. BLUES:JIMMIE GORDON
SHREVEPORT STOMP:JELLY ROLL MORTON
THINKIN' BLUES:BESSIE SMITH
SAVE IT PRETTY MAMA:LOUIS
LOVER COME BACK TO ME:MILDRED BAILEY
BESSIE COULDN'T HELP IT:LOUIS

My dad's "Nostalgia Rides Again" chart,
listing his most treasured records.

Chapter 3

Pass Out Lightly

There's nothing like learning some exceptionally cool things about your mother, and coming to realize why she was the life of every party she threw. It was the discovery of my dad's upbringing, though, that truly blew me away.

The signature stroke of his career was *Manhattan Tower*, essentially a Broadway play on vinyl, the first "concept" album ever recorded and a testament to his love for New York. He was making a ton of money in the '40s, spending it just as quickly as it arrived, and he'd make extensive visits to the city for recording dates or just plain enjoyment. Marvelous example: Through his constant visits to the jazz and blues clubs, he became enamored with an all-black group known as the Spirits of Rhythm, whose lead singer, Leo Watson, was known to have inspired Louis Armstrong.

Gor spared no expense in New York, renting out lavish suites with fabulous views, throwing parties that lasted days on end, and one night he hired the Spirits to come play for his friends. This was the life he led, hooked on the city in a manner only wealth and celebrity can provide. *Manhattan Tower*, originally seventeen minutes and then expanded into a full LP, was his expression of that lifestyle, complete with a narrator, sound effects, original songs, a full orchestra and chorus, and two lead singers: Bill Lee and Beverly. I had a terrific interview long ago with Billy Crystal's uncle, Milt Gabler, who produced countless Jenkins recordings for Decca, and he told me *Manhattan Tower* lay dormant for months, largely unrecognized, until it suddenly took off — "a revelation," he said. "All the sophisticates around town just loved it. Gordy wound up playing it on the Ed Sullivan Show (February 1950) and that was nearly five years after it was recorded."

At the height of his career — the early '50s, when at one point he'd either written or conducted five of the top 10 hits on the Billboard charts — he was known as the king of schmaltz, churning out lavish string arrangements designed, quite frankly, to get people necking on the couch. His love of the classics — Debussy, Rachmaninoff, Tchaikovsky — was well known, complete with distinct reminders in certain arrangements. By the prime of his life, with Sinatra settling for no one but Gordon Jenkins for those mournful, set-'em-up-Joe tunes, he became identified with ballads. "You want to swing, get Nelson Riddle," they'd say, and to a point, they were right. But the depth of my father's musical background was a mystery — even to me, until he was no longer around to reveal it.

There was no shortage of good music in his native St. Louis, and he grew up hearing a healthy dose of sophisticated jazz and popular music. But something was happening elsewhere, something titanic and life-changing. On the tenth of May, 1927, two days before Gor's seventeenth birthday, Louis Armstrong stepped into a Chicago studio and recorded "Potato Head Blues," unleashing a 32-bar trumpet solo that served as a wake-up call to the future. Down in New Orleans, where Armstrong was raised, they knew all about this cat. Over the decades, he routinely cut records that shook the souls of trumpet players across the world. But "Potato Head Blues" had the devastating clarity of a gunshot in the forest. If you ever watched *Boardwalk Empire*, the Martin Scorsese-inspired TV show featuring Steve Buscemi and a well-chosen cast, you're painfully familiar with a soundtrack featuring the wooden, warbling crooners of the 1920s — perfectly acceptable at the time but borderline dreadful in retrospect. Louis Armstrong set fire to all that. Rendered it useless. A single record changed everything.

"It came from out of nowhere, to shake up jazz history," wrote critic Rick Riccardi, who has dedicated his life to the art. "No one else even attempted 'Potato Head Blues' on record for decades. There are no references to Armstrong performing it live or in concert, either. It was just three sublime minutes of his life and that was it."

Some say the record turned jazz from ensemble music to a soloist's art. The actress Tallulah Bankhead said she played it in her dressing room every night during intermission while she appeared on Broadway, just to acknowledge a higher calling. Woody Allen, a devotee of Dixieland music, once declared it "one of the reasons life is worth living."

I have no idea when Gor first heard that record; it may have been several years after the recording date. But it lured him into the jazz-and-blues cauldron of the Deep South, and he never let go. By the time I came onto the scene, he had preserved a number of 78-rpm records from the '20s and '30s, but he was crafting a more grandiose plan: to collect all those records, the ones that meant the most to him, and put them on tape. He called the project "Nostalgia Rides Again" and built a mighty stash, many of them obscure recordings long forgotten by all but the aficionados. Some of the artists are quite familiar — Armstrong, Bunny Berigan, Harold Arlen, Bob Crosby, Duke Ellington — but this collection ventured deep underground: Sonny Boy Williamson, Nellie Lutcher, Cousin Joe, Tampa Red, Chippie Hill and Bumblebee Slim, with some deliciously risqué titles:

Empty Bed Blues
Pass Out Lightly
Rich Man in the Graveyard
Think You Need a Shot
Can't Get That Stuff No More
Low Down Nasty
I'll Be Glad When You're Dead

In October of 1978, one of those horrific Malibu fires swept through our neighborhood and took the house, burned it straight to the ground. About all that was left was the chimney — and my dad's separate studio, miraculously preserved. As such, "Nostalgia Rides Again" was among the survivors. I never had much use for it, figuring it was some long-irrelevant genre from another time, but I was ever so wrong. Gor had the good sense to transfer all his reel-to-reel tapes to cassettes, and finally, right around the time I turned sixty, I took it upon myself to hear every last record. This was well before I knew anything about "Potato Head Blues" or the catalyst of revolution, but to me, that record stood out above the rest. My God, what an awakening. I tried to imagine my dad's joyous reaction, so many years before. I knew he came to revere Armstrong, like a man who worships the sun, and when he got a chance to record with "Satchmo" on Decca Records in the early '50s, he was barely able to control himself. Tears streamed down his cheeks *while* he conducted the orchestra.

I'll tell you how deep this relationship went, through the words of Nick Fatool, a legendary drummer who often played in the Jenkins orchestra:

"Gordy and Louis were on the same bill together at the Paramount Theater in New York (1952). Afterward, Gordy would go down to Nick's in the Village to hear jazz, and he'd get up every morning with one hell of a hangover. Back at the Paramount, he'd stand in the wings holding Louis's handkerchiefs. And hell, Satch would sweat and spit into those things, you know. But Gordy said just holding those handkerchiefs revived him, like an electric shock. It was his way to get back."

Because of all this, I'll make a statement that might even be true: "Potato Head Blues" was Gordon Jenkins' "Shop Around."

Gordon Jenkins cracks up Sinatra,
not for the first time, around 1978.

Chapter 4

Surprise Guests

There's no way I could have known that Bob Dylan and my father would be interlocked through time, far below the surface but connected all the same.

At first, it was little more than a hilarious coincidence, the two of them simultaneously inducted into the Songwriters Hall of Fame (1982). Here we truly had the opposite ends of the spectrum: a gravel-voiced eccentric accompanying himself with a harmonica, battering down the walls of convention, and a master of elaborate orchestration with a long history of working alongside the greats.

Although the topic never came up, I'm certain my dad was repulsed by Dylan's voice. He was accustomed to Sinatra, Steve Lawrence, Mel Torme, and was unrelenting in his denigration of lesser talents.

I didn't much care for Dylan, either, at least not at the beginning, but he won me over with his lyrics — not only those that spoke for civil rights and responsible government, but those composed entirely on a whim:

Well, Shakespeare, he's in the alley
With his pointed shoes and his bells
Speaking to some French girl
Who says she knows me well
And I would send a message
To find out if she's talked
But the post office has been stolen
And the mailbox is locked

Grandpa died last week
And now he's buried in the rocks
But everybody still talks about
How badly they were shocked
But me, I expected it to happen
I knew he'd lost control
When he built a fire on Main Street
And shot it full of holes

— "Stuck Inside of Mobile with
the Memphis Blues Again"

Well, my telephone rang it would not stop
It's President Kennedy callin' me up
He said, My friend, Bob, what do we need to make
    the country grow?
I said, My friend, John, Brigitte Bardot
Anita Ekberg
Sophia Loren
Country'll grow

Now, the man on the stand he wants my vote
He's a-runnin' for office on the ballot note
He's out there preachin' in front of the steeple
Tellin' me he loves all kinds-a people
He's eatin' bagels
He's eatin' pizza
He's eatin' chitlins

Well, ask me why I'm drunk alla time
It levels my head and eases my mind
I just walk along and stroll and sing
I see better days and I do better things
I catch dinosaurs
Make love to Elizabeth Taylor
Catch hell from Richard Burton

    — "I Shall Be Free"

What nobody realized about Dylan, way back in the mid-'60s, was that he had a pop-singer's soul — or at the very least, an unspoken appreciation for the art. This came to light just recently with the release of his album *Shadows in the Night*. At the age of seventy-three, he decided to record an album of mournful ballads, all of them performed by Sinatra in the golden years, with only a handful of musicians. As critic Richard Torres wrote on firstofthemonth.org ("A website of the radical imagination"), "Most salutes center on the Chairman's work with arranger Nelson Riddle. Their collaboration during the '50s and '60s cemented Sinatra's image as the greatest manic depressive singer extant as he veered from ultra-cool swinger to broken-hearted balladeer. Not Dylan. Most of the tunes on *Shadows* come from Sinatra's work with arranger Gordon Jenkins."

For the sake of balance in my father's biography, I made certain to include the bitter admonishments of his work from Jonathan Schwartz, the popular New York disc jockey, and critic Will Friedwald, both of whom "dismissed Jenkins' work as hokey hack schmaltz," Torres wrote. "What they fail to understand is that at the heart of what they trash as classical cacophony is Sinatra singing with a fragility no other arranger consistently brought out of him. Sinatra's best work with Jenkins — *No One Cares, All Alone, September of My Years, She Shot Me Down,* and their maiden effort, *Where Are You?,* from which *Shadows* takes four of its songs — is unabashedly, unashamedly emotional."

In an interview with *AARP The Magazine* (something I usually discard in horror), Dylan said there was no sense performing songs of this nature "unless you believe the song and have lived it. You have to know something about love and loss and feel it just as much, or there's no point in doing it. People talk about Frank all the time — and they *should* talk about Frank — but he brought out the best in these guys: Billy May and Nelson Riddle or Gordon Jenkins. They worked for him in a different kind of way than they worked for other people. They gave him arrangements that are just sublime on every level. Frank sang *to* you, not at you, like so many pop singers today. I never wanted to be a singer that sings at somebody. I always wanted to sing *to* somebody."

Dylan went on to say that "you usually hear these songs with a full-out orchestra. But I was playing them with a five-piece band and didn't miss the orchestra. I didn't have a producer coming in and saying, 'Let's put strings here and a horn section there.' I wasn't even going to use keyboards or a grand piano. One of the keys was to get the piano right off the floor and not be influenced by it in any way."

Surely, Dylan was aware of the fact that my father launched America's folk-music movement, at least from a popular standpoint, although he didn't realize it at the time. Gor found himself returning to the Village Vanguard, over and over, to hear the great Pete Seeger and the Weavers perform in 1950. In those days of Communist paranoia, the Weavers were considered wild-eyed radicals, not to be trusted, and they never dreamed of recording with a major label. But Gor was a bigshot at Decca at the time, its most popular recording artist, and he insisted. "Record these people or I walk," is how it basically went down. The result was "Goodnight Irene," a million-selling No. 1 hit, and thus began a glorious procession of folk artists including the Limelighters, the Kingston Trio, Peter, Paul and Mary, Joan Baez and Dylan himself.

(It's remarkable how completely unpredictable tributes come forth. In the summer of 2015, Rolling Stones icon Keith Richards released the CD *Life Companion: 15 Tracks That Shaped the Human Riff.* These were songs from his youth, the ones that really hit home, featuring the likes of Muddy Waters, Bo Diddley and Jimmy Reed, with a little taste of the Everly Brothers and Buddy Holly, among others. The very last track is "Gordon Jenkins and his Orchestra with the Weavers." As noted in *Mojo* magazine, "Goodnight Irene" was originally recorded by Leadbelly in 1933, but "The Weavers' interpretation is included here because of Gordon Jenkins' lush orchestration, which echoes the sentimentality of Keith's emotive version. A fine end to *Life Companion.*")

Right about the time "Shadows" was released, I heard from Greil Marcus, the longtime *Rolling Stone* contributor who spent decades immersed in Dylan's work and authored *Bob Dylan by Greil Marcus: Writings 1968-2010*. He was writing a monthly column for Barnes & Noble Review and wondered if Gordon Jenkins' son might be interested in critiquing Dylan's adventure. I went through the album three times: listening to it from my perspective, then through my father's ultra-critical ear, then back to mine, and came up with this:

"I left my canvassing tools behind. I didn't want to know what any music critic felt about Dylan's project, or hear any bitter resentment over such a radical departure from the Sinatra mood. I listened to this album strictly from the perspective of being Gordon Jenkins' son — and I have to tell you, I found it quite sweet and tender.

"My father always said that he and Sinatra made *September of My Years* at exactly the right time (1965) of their lives: mid-fifties, harboring untold memories of lost love and heartbreak, but still absolutely in their prime. I'm so glad to hear Dylan, in his interviews, speak to this. At his peak, he was far too contemporary to pay attention to Sinatra. He wrote the smartest lyrics of his generation (and of many others, I might add) and spoke to the people right then and there. It seems that as a lover of words, though, he stashed certain lyrics in the back of his mind, deeply meaningful passages from songs he knew would stand up over time.

"He dug the melodies, too. And it was such a good idea to abandon any reliance upon strings, horns or even the piano. That's been done already, and quite well. Dylan went into the studio with a gifted pedal steel player, Donny Herron, who carried the instrumentals along with two guitarists, a bass player and a percussionist. The result is a decidedly unique interpretation of some classic material, and if Dylan's voice sounds a little raw, hey, the man's been belting 'em out for decades. My father used to get up and leave the room if some half-baked singer appeared on television, and Dylan's work might have driven him crazy after two or three bars. For me — and this is so crucial — the *feeling* is there, and if a Sinatra-Jenkins record strikes the image of a well-worn fellow pondering his fate at some lonesome tavern, Dylan resurrects it to perfection.

"I wonder if any of the old-school aficionados noticed a glowing tribute to my father's work at the end of *Where Are You?* Herron replicates the ending exactly: same key, the same four notes repeated, and then the finishing chord. How perfect to hear just a *touch* of the old man in there, before drifting back into Dylan's special world."

It's a shame that Sinatra and my father aren't around to get a load of Dylan's project, but Sinatra got a taste in November of 1995, when he taped a two-hour ABC telecast called "Frank Sinatra: 80 Years My Way" at the Shrine Auditorium in Los Angeles. A number of guest artists appeared, including Dylan, then fifty-four and anxious to perform a song he'd written some thirty years before. It was called "Restless Farewell," and as Torres described it, "In Sinatraspeak, a tune full of broads, bucks, booze, battles, buddies and bye-byes. Dylan's rendition of it that night was extraordinary. The sole shot of Sinatra during the performance shows his famed blue eyes glistening as he appeared to contemplate the truth — his truth — just voiced. This was Dylan and Sinatra — two outsiders, two sensitive observers, two supreme interpreters, two musical road warriors fascinated by society's losers — bonding over a tune. This was reporting. This was real. That's why Sinatra related to it. That's why the tears started to flow."

Torres mentioned the Jenkins/Weavers collaboration in his review, as well as the fact that when Harry Nilsson decided to record an album of old standards, "A Little Touch of Schmilsson in the Night," he chose my father. And that's a crazy, rollicking story in itself.

This was London, 1973, a time when Nilsson partied furiously into the night with John Lennon and Derek Taylor, the man who succeeded Brian Epstein as the so-called "fifth Beatle." Taylor was a quick-witted, highly cultured sort, fond of the musical classics, and he envisioned an album in which Nilsson would sing some decades-old standards to the accompaniment of a major orchestra. I'll never forget Derek explaining why he didn't choose Nelson Riddle: "He walked like a Republican." Something about Gor's approach struck Taylor as the perfect foil, and thus unfolded some magical sessions at Wembley Studio: Gor conducting his own arrangements for a band mostly populated by the London Symphony. (True to the British standard, they knew *all* about him; some had played on his Judy Garland dates at London's Dominion Theater in 1957.)

I had the pleasure of witnessing those sessions first-hand, and they were spectacular. When I interviewed Nilsson many years later, he described the experience as "God-like, the best album I was ever associated with. I'll stack it up against anybody's — show me what you got." And here's my point, as it connects to Motown: Sobriety was not a prerequisite.

You talk about a triple-threat performer: Nilsson spent entire days and nights indulging himself in weed, Scotch and cocaine — and I mean, *during* the recording sessions. I know my dad was appalled, but something told him to employ a long-trusted judgment: Was it working? It undeniably was. Nilsson sang magnificently — for the last time, really, in his career. He floated through an enchanted sort of dreamland each day, never screwing up in the presence of Jenkins and some of the best musicians in the world. Years later, as I spoke with Nilsson and Taylor, I learned that Harry had ventured even deeper into serious debauchery, rotting out those once-angelic vocal chords and pretty much the rest of him. Such an abbreviated life — he died at fifty-two — but never short on revelry.

I discovered something very important right then, and later on in researching my dad's life: Real genius must be tolerated. Gor was willing to overlook petulance, drunkenness and belligerence, among other annoyances, if the work was high-class. He spoke of working with Al Jolson, a fabulous entertainer and first-class jerk, in the late '30s. He conducted orchestras for Garland, who in a certain state was terrified to go on stage; my father literally left the orchestra pit to find her, grab her by the shoulders and escort her into the wings. He sailed through recording sessions with Sinatra, who was known to be rudely dismissive of bandleaders he didn't respect. "I'm a talent worshipper," Gor said on a radio interview around the late '60s. "I've got to make allowances for people with that much talent. I don't see why they've got to be like the guy who sells you the bakery stuff. People with talent are entitled to aberrations that you don't expect from a cab driver."

Make no mistake, my sportswriting career was galaxies removed from Garland and Sinatra, but

I came in close contact with the likes of Barry Bonds, Jose Canseco, John McEnroe, Tiger Woods and so many other people you'd rather not be around. Bonds turned down my interview requests so often, I decided I wouldn't talk to *him* — and didn't, for more than ten years. If there was a media crowd around Bonds, I'd go talk to the catcher. But it never stopped me from praising his otherworldly talent, casting Hall of Fame votes for him and rigorously defending that stance against the crowd of self-righteous moralists. And I thank my father for that. If anyone ever wondered why I take a rather jaded approach to drugs and sports — appreciate the entertainment, for God's sake, then kiss your wife — perhaps it's explained in these pages. It's not a terribly noble stance, rendered caustic by the grand proclamations of being "clean" on "an even playing field," but screw the even playing field. Hendrix didn't play there. Neither did Miles Davis, Billie Holiday, Louis Armstrong or a thousand great athletes over the years. Give me a little taste of whatever John Belushi and Richard Pyror were having. And I'd love to have plugged into the Motown players' state of mind as they revolutionized popular music. I'd break the bank for the price of admission.

THE MIRACLES

A TAMLA recording

SHOP AROUND

SHOP AROUND · WHO'S LOVIN' YOU
AIN'T IT BABY · THE ONLY ONE I LOVE

Smokey Robinson (center) and the Miracles
changed everything with "Shop Around."

Chapter 5

Smokey's Blow to the Heart

I knew there were elements of fantasy and pixie dust to the Motown story, but I couldn't have envisioned the logistical miracle that went down in Detroit. The common assumption would be that talented black artists came from around the country — Chicago, Nashville, Memphis, New York — to record at the Motown studios. In fact, most of its great artists were from right around the corner, the Brewster neighborhood, a rough part of town that embraced music as its salvation.

Put it this way, when it comes to my "Shop Around" hero, Smokey Robinson: One afternoon he went visiting at a friend's house, and there was a four-year-old girl playing a pretty fine piano: Aretha Franklin. About four doors down Belmont Street from the Robinson household, a girl named Diana

Ross grew up. Marvin Gaye was a neighbor, and Stevie Wonder. Good heavens. That's like discovering that Mel Brooks, Jonathan Winters, Mort Sahl, Stan Freberg and Lenny Bruce used to sit around the schoolyard cracking each other up.

"There was music everywhere," Robinson recalled in a TV interview. "It was very vigorous, a lot of hustle and bustle going on. Singing groups on every corner. In that neighborhood, you were either in a group or a gang — or both. I had a wonderful time growing up, and I was very spiritual. I didn't do drugs or anything like that. My friends would do things that I wouldn't do, because I felt like God was watching me."

William Robinson got his nickname from his uncle and godfather, Claude, who loved taking the kid to cowboy movies. "From the time I could talk until I was about seven or eight, I wanted to be a cowboy when I grew up. After a while my uncle came up with a great cowboy name for me: Smokey Joe. That's what people called me until I was about twelve, when I dropped the Joe off and just became Smokey. I've heard that story about how I was light-skinned and my uncle never wanted me to forget I was black. But that's not where the name came from."

I felt a remote but powerful connection to Smokey when I learned more about his upbringing. His dad wasn't around much, but his mom filled the house with music of all kinds: B.B. King, Muddy Waters, John Lee Hooker, Sarah Vaughan, Billy Eckstine, the great Gershwin tunes, Bessie Smith, Charlie Parker, Miles Davis, Tchaikovsky, Mozart, just a constant swirl of excellence. That was the pristine climate of my own childhood. I'm sure my parents would have loved knowing Smokey's mom. "And for me, man, it was 24-7," he said. "I had a great dose of everything."

The child had a gift. He was a natural wordsmith. The elegance of rhyme and rhythm came easy to him, and he was writing songs before he even started school. "The first time anybody actually heard my stuff, I was six," he said. "One of my teachers had written some music that she played before and after a school play. I went and asked her, 'Miss Campbell, can I write some words to that song?' Of course, she said, so I did, and she let me sing 'em at the performance. My mom was in the audience, and that night you would have thought I was Cole Porter. That's how she reacted."

When Smokey was ten, his mother died of a brain hemorrhage. "Like the end of the world for me," he said. "That's a heavy blow, at ten years old, to think I wasn't gonna have my mom any more. But you know, you go on. My older sister, Geraldine, came back to live in our house, and there were about eleven of us altogether. She was a lot like my mom, and she raised me."

It wasn't long before Smokey began singing together with a couple of local boys, Pete Moore and Bobby Rogers. He was fifteen when he formed a five-boy group of Northern High School kids called the Chimes. That group eventually became the Matadors, rehearsing in the Rogers' basement, where Bobby's sister, Claudette, liked to hang around. Turned out she could sing a little bit, too, and when the Matadors became the Miracles in 1957, she was part of the group, joining Moore, Ronnie White, her brothers Bobby and Emerson, and the seventeen-year-old Smokey (two years later, he and Claudette were married).

Robinson's songwriting was nothing short of prolific, but the group wasn't getting anywhere. Then came an audition, in the heart of Detroit, with some high-powered record executives. "It didn't go well," Claudette said. "We sang about five songs that Smokey had written, but they said something like,

'There's a girl in the background, and we've already heard that from the Platters, and we don't need another group like that.' It was total rejection."

It so happened that a teenage songwriting wizard named Berry Gordy was in the room as a talent scout. He was already a force in the industry, having written "Lonely Teardrops," "Reet Petite" (great name) and several other hits for the fabulous Jackie Wilson. "I didn't pay any attention to this guy because he looked about sixteen, and wasn't a whole lot older than that," Robinson said. "But when the audition was over, he stopped us in the hallway."

As Robinson recalls it:

"Hey, man, where'd you get those songs?" Gordy wondered.

"They're mine — I wrote 'em," Robinson said.

"You wrote all those? 'Cause a couple of 'em I liked. You got any more songs?"

"I do," said Robinson, who carried around a loose-leaf notebook with "about a hundred" songs he'd written.

"Well, listen, man, I like your voice," Gordy said. "Nobody sounds like you."

"Thank you," Smokey said. "And what's your name?"

Robinson was floored by the response. "From the time I was little, I always looked at the records to see who wrote the songs," he said years later. "I knew everything about Jackie Wilson; he was my idol. Now I'm meeting the guy who wrote so many of his hits? I was flabbergasted."

That, right there, was the birth of Motown. It was 1957 and nothing would ever be the same in Detroit, or anywhere else. The two struck up a friendship and began comparing notes. Within a year, Gordy had founded the company, as well as a subsidiary label, Tamla, on which the Miracles recorded many of their hits. "Berry taught me how to write songs professionally," Robinson said. "I had my songs all rhymed up; I could always rhyme stuff. But they didn't make sense. I'd have like five songs in one, 'cause the idea kept changin'. He told me that good songs have a beginning, a middle and an end that ties it all together, and people can take something from it."

Like so many Motown groups to follow, the Miracles were smooth and polished, stylish dancers and immaculately dressed. Watching so many groups today, you get the idea they'd prefer to look as dreadful as humanly possible. You'll see a guy's pants that drag a good six inches' worth along the floor (always tidy on the streets of dog shit) and peak around the upper thigh ("So how's it going with your privates?"). The no-shirt look brings that special touch of conceit. Motown was all about class, an extension of the Count Basie-Duke Ellington days, when high fashion blended so marvelously with sophisticated sounds. Watching the Motown groups perform on TV shows like *American Bandstand* and *Shindig*, I always felt those lucky kids in the audience were in the presence of royalty.

The Miracles had a couple of modest hits, "Got a Job" (released on Robinson's eighteenth birthday in 1958) and "Bad Girl," before striking it rich with "Shop Around," all about a mother's advice to play the field, live a little, before settling down with someone. These were words young Smokey himself received, before his mother passed away, and he once told National Public Radio that he wrote the song in about twenty minutes, that "sometimes the songs just flowed out of me, and those were often the hits."

"Shop Around" was the first No. 1 R&B hit (No. 2 on the pop charts) for Berry Gordy and his Tamla/ Motown empire. Robinson had written the song for another Motown artist, Barrett Strong, but Gordy convinced him to record it with the Miracles and have Smokey's wife, Claudette, sing lead. "It was a slower and more bluesy number when they first recorded it," according to songfacts.com. "It was released as a single, but late one night, Gordy woke up Robinson with a phone call announcing he'd thought up a different arrangement and called the group into the studio to record it." Excellent call, sir. With Smokey on lead, the hit version was recorded around 3 a.m., and it *cooks.*

I came across a review in allmusic.com by Richie Unterberger, who wrote that "though Robinson might be more known for romantic crooning than tough rock 'n' roll, he could also deliver a lyric with ingratiating assertiveness, hitting some particularly impressive high notes at the end of the bridge. The song's vocal roots in doo wop and gospel were there to hear, but really it was the first prominent example of the new kind of soul music Motown pioneered; as much pop as gospel, catchy but tough, jazzy in arrangement but reined in to support rock 'n' roll hooks."

That's all very nice, but I can't analyze music from a critic's standpoint. I don't really analyze it at all; it either works or it doesn't. You know when something strikes a penetrating blow to the heart, and that's how I felt as a twelve-year-old, music-wise kid listening to "Shop Around."

When I became of age
My mother called me to her side
She said, son, you're growing up now
Pretty soon you'll take a bride

That was Smokey's intro, a beautiful setup, with some moody horns in the background. After about a three-second pause, the tempo jumps and the man goes off. I've included all of his inflections here, because they're so crucial to the impact:

And then she said,
Just because you've become a young man, now
There's still some things that you don't under-
*   stand, now*
Before you ask some girl for her hand, now
Keep your freedom for as long as you can, now
My mama told me
You better shop around
Uh-whoa yay-uh, you better shop around

You can hear the rest of the Miracles in the background now, especially Claudette, now Smokey's lover, and what a lovely addition. OK, so the Platters had a female background vocalist amongst a few guys. What, that's the last we'll hear of it? Motown turned this into a staple, with Robinson right at the forefront. He and Claudette would have their problems later in life, but in 1960 they were cookin', and believe me, that hits home. My father often tried to describe the feeling of conducting an orchestra with his girlfriend (and later wife) belting out solos right in front of him — and he really couldn't. There just aren't any words for something like that.

It's so important to realize that "Shop Around" was a brand-new sound, just like Ray Charles' "I Got a Woman," James Brown's "Out of Sight" or Stevie Wonder's "Fingertips." There was so much passion and excitement in Robinson's voice, a burst of classy, honest enthusiasm, and like Marvin Gaye, Smokey sang like a drummer. He'd toss in a vocal fill (like all those "nows") to keep the rhythm in place, or take it to a fresh new place. Like right here, as the song continues, he throws in three notes before the actual lyrics begin, and it means *everything*, just changes the whole deal;

Ah-ah-ahhh, There's some things that I want you
to know, now
Uh-Just as sure as the wind's gonna blow, now
The women come and the women gonna go, now
Before you tell 'em that you love 'em so, now
My mama told me
You better shop around
Oh, yeah [gets five notes out of that last word;
pure magic]
You better shop around

And the bridge, with more crucial single-note fills:

Uh-Try to get yourself a bargain, son
Don't be sold on the very first one
Uh-Pretty girls come a dime a dozen
Uh-Try to find who who's gonna give you
true lovin'
Before you take a girl and say I do, now
Uh-Make sure she's in love with uh-you, now
My mama told me
You better shop around

See, you're just not walking away from Smokey
Robinson. Nobody could cover this song, either, not

with any sense of dignity. Trying to copy Smokey's fills would fall somewhere between blasphemy and misdemeanor. You won't find those "*uh*s" in any strict representation of the lyrics, and I know they look clumsy in print, but he put them there, right on the spot. Sweet percussion from the vocalist.

Then comes a tasty little sax solo, which I have to admit was somewhat rare from Motown in those days. I don't know the man's name — for years, the record-buying public had no idea who was playing behind the Motown stars — but one saxophonist sounded as if he'd left his horn out in a blizzard for a few days (hear it on "You Lost the Sweetest Boy" or "Helpless," among others). Not this man, though. He carved a jazzy path to Smokey's return, and I can't even explain how that happens (this hard-core inspection is a bit new to me). Technically it's "Oh, yeah," but he gets about ten syllables out of it, and "yeah" sounds more like "hey" at the finish. All of it essential, because he's ahead of you. Smokey was ahead of everything back then: the lyrics, the band, the public, and especially his time.

Oh, yeah [Simplified] *Try to get yourself*
    a bargain, son
Don't be sold on the very first one
    [five notes' worth]
Uh-Pretty girls come a dime a dozen
Uh-Gotta find one who's gonna GIVE
    [fairly yelps it out] *you true lovin'*

Before you take a girl and say I do, now
Make sure she's in love with-uh you, now
Make sure that her love is true, now
I hate to see you feelin' sad and blue, now
My mama told me
You better shop around

And now the rideout, with great stuff from a master of soulful rhyme:

Uh-huh, Don't let the first-uh one gitcha
Oh, no, 'cause I don't wanna see her wit' cha
Ah-uh-huh, Before you let her hold you tight
Uh-yay-yeah, Make sure she's all right
    [five notes as one]
Uh-huh, Before you let her take your hand, my son
Understand, my son

Be a man, my son
I know you can, my son [a couple of
   fleeting words in the fadeout]

And all around the country, people picked themselves up off the floor.

As Claudette recalled, "The city of Detroit had a
rhythm to it in those days, such a wonderful place to
be. 'Shop Around' being the first million-seller really
put Motown on the air waves, really put it out there
so that people had a *feeling.* There's a new sheriff
in town."

Berry Gordy was so right: Nobody sounded like
Smokey Robinson, not ever. From that point on,
the hits flowed with stunning quality and precision.
Between April 1962 and October '66, the Miracles
cranked out "I'll Try Something New," "You've Really
Got a Hold On Me," "Mickey's Monkey," "That's What
Love Is Made Of," "Ooo Baby Baby," "The Tracks of
My Tears," "Going to a-Go-Go," and "I'm the One You
Need" on Gordy's Tamla label, essentially keeping it
going by themselves. Audiences wept and swooned
in the presence of Smokey's silky ballads. He had a
knack for finding that precious gray area in a vocal,
somewhere between elation and regret, and it just

knocked everybody out. Gordy once said Smokey was "probably responsible for more babies in that time than any single person." And somewhere along the line, a vastly impressed Bob Dylan declared Smokey "America's greatest living poet."

What struck me with equal force, in retrospect, was learning of Robinson's extreme generosity when it came to recording hits. He had a hand in most of them, all down the line in the Motown stable. He wrote huge hits for the Temptations, Mary Wells, the Four Tops, Marvin Gaye and the rest, pushing them all toward greatness. He was in essence the king of Motown, a master of production (and eventually a company vice president), but he truly loved having other artists record his songs, watching them come to life in ways distinct to the artist in question.

"I'd have to say Marvin was my favorite, although I loved 'em all," he said. "You have to remember that in those days, there was only one recording track. The singer, the band, the mixing, it's all happening right now. They don't record like that any more, man. They don't even see each other. They'll come in to record stuff at a different time, a different day, a different week. Back then, you had to be *on* it. And everybody who's gonna be on that recording had better be in the studio right then. Well, Marvin was always late. When he came into the studio, the door was hittin' him on the ankle. But he was my brother. We hung out together all the time. So if we had a session that started at 8, I'd tell Marvin 6:30, so he'd be there at 8:30. And he still might be a little bit late.

"*However.* He'd come in for a song he'd never heard before. I'd sit at the piano and show it to him. And he'd sing it in a way I never could have imagined. He'd sing that song like he knew it before he got there. Like *he* wrote it. I used to tell him all the time, man, you just Marvin-ized my song. 'Cause that's what he did. Marvin was *awesome.*"

As Motown took the nation by storm, "People were comin' into Detroit from all over the world," he said, "thinking that if you if you came to record here, you'd get the Motown sound because that's where it was, lurking in the air somewhere. What they didn't realize is that the Motown sound is the *people. We* are the Motown sound. And, man, we bombarded them with hits. Over and over again."

In those days, it was customary for record labels to push hard for exposure, paying off disc jockeys to get songs on the air. "Payola, they called it," Robinson said. "We never had to go through that. We had a period of time where the DJs were calling us so they'd have the record first. Motown was a phenomenon, a once-in-a-lifetime thing. Nothing like that had ever happened in the music business, and I doubt seriously if it will happen again."

Second from left, with soul man Lyle Spencer (center),
on the Samohi sports staff at Santa Monica High, 1966.

Chapter 6

Motown Explored

I was thirteen years old when I learned a basic truth about the music business. It was sort of like experiencing a slice of heaven, then being safely dispatched back to Earth. It was Hollywood, 1962, and I walked out of a Jenkins-Sinatra recording session knowing I'd never be quite the same.

My dad had assembled a forty-odd-piece orchestra with all of his favorite players, the best in town, from the oboe to the French horns to the harp. They had rehearsed the album (*All Alone*) but not extensively; the talent and sight-reading ability in that room was just that great. Sinatra hadn't rehearsed at all. He didn't believe in it. He knew the songs, and the arrangements, and he didn't feel like wasting his voice on something that would vanish into thin air. He tended to absolutely nail it, immediately, and if there was the slightest glitch in the orchestra, even something imperceptible to the layman's ear, Gor or Frank would bring things to a halt.

It's difficult to remember exactly how the session went down, but I distinctly remember them knocking off one tune in a single take. Others stuttered and stopped, but never to the point of tedium. The entire twelve-song album was recorded in just three days, and it's not as if they were staying up late. Gor and Frank were adamant about launching that cocktail hour on time, and a lot of those band members felt the same way. Take care of unfinished business tomorrow, if it even exists.

What I learned is that the professionals do it right, the first time. None of the musicians get lost, space out, show up late to the studio. Presented with a piece of music, they hastily grasp its every nuance. It's a hell of a lofty standard, and as the years went on, I could only lament the sorry state of rock-band recording sessions. Some of them went down smoothly with elite studio musicians (such as L.A.'s legendary "Wrecking Crew"), but others were little more than a joke: weeks on end in an attempt to produce a single album, featuring piles of cocaine, ludicrous dialogue and maybe one good idea.

I wasn't listening to Sinatra, Tony Bennett or Henry Mancini in my teens, but I came to value really good musicianship, the kind you can spot without fail. That's why I became so enamored with Motown, and later Stax, out of Memphis. It's been so gratifying in recent years to learn that these indeed were the bad-ass players of their day: James Jamerson, Benny Benjamin, Booker T. Jones, Steve Cropper. I've learned, also, that the likes of Smokey Robinson and Otis Redding wouldn't have it any other way. And if for some reason any of those singers couldn't make the gig, the band could carry a show on pure instrumentals.

At Santa Monica High in the mid-'60s, I'd get into arguments about who was really dominating the music scene. I'd vigorously defend Motown against the Beatles or the Beach Boys in debates that never really got settled. I knew my fellow students would run out of wisdom if we got into true musicianship, but these were civil discussions, allowing for the possibility that your antagonist might be making a few good points. It struck me, too, that maybe one out of twenty high-school friends had heard of Gordon Jenkins. Moms and dads? Different story. But that worked for me: a famous father who wasn't all that famous. And I knew that when I walked out of that Sinatra recording session, it was an honor to last a lifetime.

Right now? I'd make a simple request — to go back in time. Put me in a corner of the Motown recording studio, invisible, privileged beyond words.

The scene was Detroit in the 1950s, gritty and raw but with a thriving automobile industry that lured thousands of black families from the South, anxious to better their lives. Berry Gordy was one of history's true visionaries, knowing he could tap into the city's vast well of talent if he could catch a couple of breaks. Thanks to an $800 loan from his family, he bought a used, 1939 Western Electric two-track recording console and opened up his own publishing company and record label. The entire operation was housed in a basement studio at 2648 West Grand Boulevard, a totally nondescript setting not unlike the Stax headquarters in Memphis, under the marquee of the old Capitol Theater at 926 East McLemore.

Walking by, you'd have no idea what was taking place inside. It seems almost inconceivable in retrospect, but within the narrow confines of that studio, with its wooden floor and neighborhood-style acoustics, a certain sound was born — never to be duplicated. Motown grew into the most successful African-American-owned business in the country, and in those tempestuous times, it made contributions to the civil-rights movement that cannot be measured.

In a stifling climate of scorn and repression, with full-scale rioting in the major cities, here came a bunch of polished, supremely talented black artists, drawing upon contemporary themes — lost love, dance away your cares, found my baby at last — but adding essential touches of crackling rhythm and jazz. (It's so curious: Back then, against America's backdrop of hatred, the lyrics were innocent and endearing, full of hope. Decades later, in a far more enlightened culture, super-wealthy performers spewed anger and resentment, discarding even the hint of melody. Never absent: the element of pride.)

It's stunning to consider that in drawing largely from Detroit's working-class neighborhoods, Gordy came up with professional and brilliantly confident performers, one after another, ready to impress the most strident critics and knock the doors off a crowded hall. I learned later that he employed renowned choreographers and artist-development classes, taught by one Maxine Powell, to impart lessons in media relations and etiquette. It was rare to hear that any Motown artist had been arrested, beaten down by drugs or cast in a negative light. There was torment behind the scenes, all about unpaid royalties and other injustices, but they always seemed gloriously above the fray.

As for those backup musicians — the Funk Brothers, so deeply explored in the television documentary *Standing in the Shadows of Motown*, it was quite a different story.

Basically, these guys lived to get high and play jazz. Almost to a man, they were packing heat in case somebody got a bit too riled. But they made sweet music together, and they laughed a lot, and their talent was the worst-kept secret in black Detroit. By night, they played jazz clubs: Chit Chat, Blues Unlimited, High Chaparral and Twenty Grand. That was their first love, and if any club could score all of them at once, it would be one hell of a night.

More often than not, the Motown sessions went down *after* the jazz gigs: smoke-filled affairs around two or three in the morning. That was just about right for these nocturnal cats, and they tended to favor a little boost: alcohol, weed, and in some cases, heroin, bringing to light a basic truth: Few elements in life can deter the natural musician. The pretenders claim to play better when they're loaded, as if to carry on some Hendrix-Charlie Parker-Ray Charles tradition, but it's always a lie, instantly exposed. For the great ones, hell, bring it on. Let's see what you've got inside that case. Maybe we'll feel just a little bit better. We'll still lay down that track in one take.

Everything was cut live in Motown's basement: no over-dubbing or last-minute inserts. If someone made a mistake, everyone would have to go back and do it all over again. Not that it ever became much of an issue. On good nights in Detroit, with the vocalist, backup singers and band in seamless cohesion, Motown could crank out three or four songs — very possibly *hit* songs — in a three-hour session, invariably backed by the percussion of people stomping on plywood boards, clapping hands, snapping fingers or slapping knees alongside Benny Benjamin, the innovative jazz drummer whose signature "pickups" became a staple of the Motown sound.

Decades would pass before even the most devoted fans could identify the session players. There was no such thing as album credits back then, making it all a complete mystery (except in England, where fans always seemed to know everything; the Funk Brothers would get off the plane and hear people shouting their names). The first session players to become stars were Booker T's guys — notably Steve Cropper, the superlative guitarist behind Sam and Dave, Carla Thomas and the rest of the Stax stable — and it wasn't until the late '60s that the major labels changed their policy and began acknowledging backup musicians.

What amazes people today, looking back, is how Motown produced a rich, unmistakable sound in such tight quarters. It was never reproduced, not exactly, nor did any of those people wish they could do it all over again with modern equipment. Joe Hunter, Motown's first important bandleader and pianist, once wrote that it was "awesome how they could get a lock-step interaction going. It would baffle today's computer experts. High-tech music couldn't compete with these guys when they got an honest and true groove going. There has never been and never will be a machine that could possibly have that much soul."

Guitarist Joe Messina was Italian, "but we forgot he was Italian," said Robert White, also a guitarist. "He was a black guy with a white face." One drummer, Pistol Allen, was said to be the only man in the world capable of cutting a perfect track while reading a racing form at the same time. Marvin Gaye had grown up as a drummer and he sang that way, with fabulous rhythm and phrasing (once he'd performed "Hitch Hike," that was it; no covers allowed). Stevie Wonder was in the neighborhood, for crying out loud, and he signed up when he was eleven, a few years before the "Fingertips" recording announced him to the world. Nobody ever sounded like Walter Ward, the scratchy-voiced anchor of the Olympics, best known for the original "Good Lovin'," or Major Lance on "Come See." (I've got Lance on my list of the world's greatest soul hummers, along with Edwin Starr and Tina Turner.) Smokey Robinson's vocals blew everyone away, but *his* guy was Levi Stubbs, of the Four Tops. The studio launched a memorable procession of duets: Gaye and Mary Wells, Gaye and Tammi Terrell, and on other labels, Fontella Bass and Bobby McClure, Betty Everett and Jerry Butler, Dinah Washington and Brook Benton. All of it passes the ultimate test, losing not a bit of magic over time.

I developed wild crushes on some of the performers, and in those days of limited television exposure, it came mostly from my imagination. I told myself I *had* to meet Kim Weston, who sang "Helpless," and Brenda Holloway from "When I'm Gone." I decided I would someday propose to Veronica Bennett, of the Ronettes, so devastatingly bad-girl sexy on "Do I Love You," and when she married Phil Spector, my crush was crushed. I mean, ground-breaking engineer, the whole "Wall of Sound" thing, but *wow*, what a creep. He wound up tormenting and threatening to kill Ronnie (as she was later known) as he sank deeper into eccentricity, and I forever wished the very worst upon him.

"Girl groups" still exist, but they measure poorly against the Ronettes, the Shirelles, the Marvelettes, Martha and the Vandellas or the Royalettes. Gene Chandler did a record called "Nothing Can Stop Me," and one of his backup singers stood out so clearly, I couldn't get her out of my mind. I still can't. Motoring down the highway, hearing her "Yeah, yeah, yeah," I still desperately need to know what she looked like. (If you're still around, dearest, know that you are well remembered.)

Then there was the fabled Stax horn section — the Memphis Horns, as they were known, a six-man ensemble that eventually dwindled to just two: Wayne Jackson on trumpet and Andrew Love on tenor sax. One white, the other black, both raised in Memphis and destined to perform heart-warming charts of exquisite simplicity. Who in the hell even knew who these guys were? That was the great secret of soul music in the '60s. Motown's bass player was a mystery to listeners, as well, but not to the R&B community. James Jamerson was an innovator — along the lines of Charlie Parker and John Coltrane, to hear some tell it — and it seems evident that he deeply influenced *every* bass player who would follow.

"He's really the father of the modern-day bass player," said Smokey Robinson. "He had the purest fingering — all his notes were true and pure. No matter how fast he was playing them or whatever rhythmic pattern he was doing, you could hear the whole note. That was a big part of his sound. Even today, nobody plays like that."

Jamerson's style was in essence a "walking" bass line, following the tune in a rapid-fire rhythm all his own. He did it with just a single finger, and it wasn't as if he had anything written down. He was a legendary sight reader who had perfect pitch, learned his parts instantly and soared into flights of fancy, always in precise concert with the piece's basic structure. It was an entirely new sound, and later as I began traveling through Bay Area music circles and getting to know some of the best bass players — Rocco Prestia, Steve Evans, the late Jon Knight, Karl Sevareid — I discovered that they were all Jamerson disciples.

"He was the first *melodic* electric bass player," said jazz icon Stanley Clarke. "His lines were melodies in themselves, and very difficult to replicate. Like on 'Bernadette' (by the Four Tops) — the bass on that thing is *serious.* There's still guys today who can't play that one."

Jamerson grew up in South Carolina as an admirer of gospel, jazz and the blues, all coming his way via radio or neighborhood gatherings in the late '40s and '50s. He had a speech impediment and was extremely shy about expressing himself, preferring a big upright bass as his vehicle. He wasn't much for school, but then again, what he produced from that instrument could not be taught. He was imparting his own education. By

1962, as Motown was taking off, he had switched over to a Fender Precision bass, the only model he would own for decades. His imagination ran wild as he studied exotic styles from Africa, Cuba, India and the Far East; you never knew what brand of influence crept into his playing, only that it was singular and essential.

From what I've read, he was a kindly man by nature but likely to do a 180-degree turn after a few drinks. He always kept a bottle of Metaxa (a Greek brandy) in his case, and the higher he got, the more he revealed his dark side, an inner turmoil that found him getting into fights and flashing a revolver to make a point. But he *always* could play, first time through, no screw-ups. It's said that Robinson and Gaye wouldn't go through with a session if Jamerson wasn't around, and it so happened that when Gaye was laying down tracks for his *What's Going On* album, Jamerson had been on a weeklong drinking binge. Unexpectedly, Gaye dropped by a club where Jamerson was playing and asked if he'd come by the studio. Which was all very nice, except that Jamerson was so hammered, he was unable to sit upright in his chair. Legend has it he recorded one of those tracks — and, of course, nailed it — while lying flat on his back.

The Motown name persevered for decades, but never in that pulsating groove it established from 1960 through '71. Hollywood was always an option for a label so fabulously successful, and in 1972, Motown moved its base to Los Angeles. Inevitable, and really quite sad. For a while, they considered dismantling the entire setup and reassembling it out West, but that was hardly realistic. I lost interest altogether, focusing on the dynamic new sounds coming out of the R&B world, particularly Tower of Power and Cold Blood so close to home.

What I love about Motown's golden era, and why I turn to it time and again, is the depth of its appeal. I could spend months just focusing on the backup singers, or the funky-sounding saxophone, or the endearing simplicity of Messina's rhythm guitar. Just lately it's been all James Jamerson. For most of my life, I preferred the "treble" setting on a listening device, just to avoid an overbearing bass (today, as some loser drives down the street with a rap-style bass pounding at 28 on a scale of 10, I retreat in terror). It's quite the opposite with Jamerson. He was never over-miked or even featured; he just kept it all together in the background. So instead of leaning toward the "T" on the audio-tuning dial, I've got it way over to the left, on "B," where the man comes to life. Such an easy adjustment, and such a pleasure.

**The young Steve Cropper, about to build
the foundation for Stax records.**

Chapter 7

Las Vegas, and the Search for Steve Cropper

More than a half-century had passed since I visited Las Vegas. The experience was more than a shock. I felt as if I'd landed in another country, or perhaps the planet Opulence. After four days, I'd reached a state of depression that could only be cured by one thing: soul-stirring music. Nostalgia wasn't quite cutting it.

There wasn't much to see around Vegas in the spring of 1958, when my father wrote the words and music to a hit show at the Tropicana. A couple of resorts had high-rise looks, but most everything else was low to the ground, no more than two stories high. Driving along the strip, there were majestic views of the distant mountains — and with a slight veer off the road, you'd be looking at a vast expanse of Nevada desert.

It all seemed astoundingly lavish at the time. There was no place in the world like Las Vegas, but at least you could get a handle on the place. When the Tropicana opened in April of '57, it was only the thirteenth resort/casino on the strip, joining the likes of the Desert Inn, Thunderbird, Silver Slipper, Sahara, Sands and Riviera.

I'm pretty sure you could fit all of that into to-day's Caesar's Palace. Walking along the Strip in 105-degree heat in the summer of 2015, I could see it in the near distance — but every time I drew near, another gigantic Caesar's building loomed behind it. I swear, the closer I got to the damn place, the farther away it got. (I wonder how many folks actually marvel at those pasty-white statues of ancient Romans cradling scrolls and harps. And who are those bronzed bodybuilders hanging out on the street corner, wearing only sandals, a loincloth and a facial shield? Are we in a new scene from *Spartacus*?)

What an absurdly far cry from '58, when my dad arranged for a family weekend in Vegas. Staying at the Tropicana, all of nine years old, I remember the heat, the slot machines, the showgirls by the pool (a rather distinct memory, that one). I was much too young to get into the show, called "Tropicana Holiday," with its saucy numbers and high-rolling climate. I learned later that the place had been opened by Monte Proser, the man who built and ran the Copacabana in New York before the club's heavy mob influence, fronted by Frank Costello, ran him out. I guess Proser couldn't quite shake the man, for Costello barely escaped assassination years later over gambling issues from the Tropicana.

In any case, Gordon Jenkins was right in the middle of all this — and feeling quite at home. There was a lot of big money floating around, and Sinatra told me Gor routinely bet "a bundle" at the roulette wheel, sometimes nailing a massive score, more often losing his shirt. But that's the great thing about the music business; there's always a new shirt. The great entertainers just have to keep working, and the coin comes rolling in.

I could go on describing the Vegas club scene back then, but the cover of *Tropicana Holiday* — the album my father conducted, featuring twelve of his original songs — does a much better job, showing a bunch of bawdy showgirls in preparation backstage. The famously chesty Jayne Mansfield played "Trixie

Divoon" in the show, big-boobing about with her husband, Mickey Hargitay, and generally thrilling the alcohol-sodden gents in the audience. In a classic review of the show, *Variety* wrote that Mansfield "makes no pretense at any particular talent other than scenic value."

That show caused quite a stir. The *Las Vegas Review-Journal* called it "by far the most ambitious display of breathtaking beauty and music ever assembled under one roof in Las Vegas." On the back of the Capitol album cover, the liner notes suggest that "it remained for Gordon Jenkins, the outstanding modern composer and lyricist, to give Las Vegas its first musical comedies, styled for Broadway, yet written expressly for the Tropicana hotel."

You might be wondering how this has any possible connection with Steve Cropper, the master rhythm guitarist of Stax records. Merely this: On my last day in Vegas, there to cover Summer League basketball, it hit me. The Strip has a soundtrack. It changes every few yards, but it is relentless: inside the casino, the hotel lobby, the restaurant, by the pool, on the street as it flows out of each establishment. The sound I most remembered from Vegas was that constant pull of a slot-machine lever, but that's a distant memory now. What good is a slot machine if you can't yank the lever, or watch a bunch of silver dollars crash into a silver bin? Now it's just music, everywhere, none of it particularly good.

Back in the Bay Area, I couldn't wait to fire up some Stax, the record company that stole my attention from Motown during my collegiate years in Berkeley. I wanted to delve back into two incisive books on that era: Peter Guralnick's *Sweet Soul Music: Rhythm and Blues and the Southern Dream of Freedom* and Rob Bowman's *Soulsville U.S.A.: The Story of Stax Records.* I wanted to leave the tacky Vegas scene behind and imagine myself in Memphis, mid-'60s, time-traveling once again as an invisible observer inside the studio. I'd be hearing Otis Redding, Sam and Dave, Carla Thomas, with Cropper setting the pace and occasionally just settling in with Booker T. and the MG's, the finest R&B instrumental ensemble of them all.

As much as a fine Motown record could lift a person's spirit, there was something deeper going on with Stax. Perhaps it is best explained by Redding's voice, a life-changing experience for anyone familiar with the history of soul-music vocals. He was just an entirely different musician, not only in terms of his passion and phrasing but the way he took command of an entire recording session, right down to the horn charts. Stax records produced a distinctly Southern sound, connecting not at all with Detroit, and to give you some idea of the contrast, *Sweet Soul Music* covers 405 pages with only *one* mention of Motown in the index. No slights or denigration intended; the Stax experience was simply a world apart. It was raw, it was pure, and it stood proudly on its own, not an easy achievement during the ascent of James Brown (another of my all-time favorites and a different story altogether).

As I tried to draw timelines to my own experience, I found it sort of cool that the Stax label was launched in 1960, the same year "Shop Around" was released. And there was a soul-music record store involved, similar in concept to the one that changed my life in Santa Monica. Big difference, though: I was a white kid discovering a haven of African-American culture in a mostly Caucasian town. Satellite Records, adjacent to the Stax studio, was run by white folks in a predominantly black neighborhood.

Memphis was ardently segregated at that time, and it remains a miracle of the music business that

Jim Stewart and his sister, Estelle Axton, got involved. They were bankers by trade, raised on country music, and although Jim played some fiddle on the side, "I had no desire to start Stax records," he said. "I had scarcely seen a black until I was grown. I just wanted to to be involved in music, one way or the other."

The old Capitol Theater had been vacated on McLemore Street, and for a hundred bucks a month, they paid the rent. Estelle took out a second mortgage on her home so they could buy an Ampex monaural recorder (then and for decades the finest brand). The theater was much too large to house an intimate recording studio, so they converted the old popcorn/candy stand area into the Satellite Records shop. They weren't kidding around, either. To satisfy the curious folks coming in for a look, they managed to secure every R&B 45 they could find — even the most obscure labels. And then there was magic: budding musicians stopped by, many of whom (including Booker T. Jones, William Bell and songwriter David Porter) were bound for greatness on the Stax label. "I was there from the beginning," Jones said. "I would just hang around pretending to look at the records, but I was really just listening to what was going on behind that curtain separating the store from the studio. Most all of our musical ideas and influences came out of that little record shop in the first couple of years."

Soon the theater's tattered marquee had a brand-new handle — "Soulsville, U.S.A" — and whatever took place on the street, Satellite Records stood for harmonious integration. A couple of Memphis-raised white kids, Cropper and bassist Donald "Duck" Dunn, became regulars, knowing they simply *had* to become part of the proceedings, for the music was in their blood.

At the beginning, it wasn't so easy. The really good live music was going down at a certain all-black nightclub across the river in West Memphis, and it was said that the talented young white kids ventured into the parking lot, where they could sit in their cars and hear the music pulsating into the night air. That wasn't quite good enough for Cropper and Dunn, however. "We just went right in," Cropper recalled. "Even when we were fifteen, we looked twelve, and they didn't care. We never asked any questions, we just walked up and said we wanted to go in. Just to listen."

Maybe this makes no sense, but in my mind, if you could picture a white guitarist with enough

confidence, style and talent to play rhythm behind Otis Redding, he would look *exactly* like Steve
Cropper in the 1960s. From the moment he heard
black gospel music, "right around the sixth grade"
over the WDIA radio waves, his life's mission was set.
"It just blew me away," he said, and from that point,
his transition into Southern-style R&B couldn't have
been more natural.

To this day, I idolize Cropper and how beautiful-
ly he molded Stax's instrumental foundation. Lord
knows it was a time of revolution for the electric guitar — Jimi Hendrix, Jimmy Page, Eric Clapton, just
let your mind take over from there — but Cropper
wasn't headed that way. It wasn't in his personality
to blow everyone's mind with a bombastic solo, or to
even attempt such a thing. "I don't care about being
center stage," he said. "I'm a band member, always
been a band member. I never liked to get away from
the rhythm too much. The whole bottom falls out."

As it developed, Stax wasn't about solos of any
kind. Rarely did they occur, on any instrument.
Cropper was looking for a crisp, razor-sharp sound
that generally landed right on the beat, basically
letting everyone know that this track was *tight* and
there would be no loose ends. The author Guralnick

marveled at Cropper's "lean, slashing" sound, not unlike "a jagged tin can being scraped with a pocket knife." One Stax-produced critique said his tone "has a metallic ferocity, yet his playing is always sparse and pervaded with a feeling of suspense."

So glorious. As a listener, I could get plenty sophisticated if the occasion demanded. I've memorized symphonic passages and I could sing you the frenetic opening of Charlie Parker's "Ornithology" (badly, but right on time). I didn't want any sweeping gestures from Cropper. I had the pocket knife ready. I'd turn the audio dial to maximum treble, just to make that guitar as lean and slashing as it could be.

It all started in 1962, when Cropper and Jones locked into a jam-session groove that became "Green Onions." That struck Cropper as "just about the best damn instrumental I'd heard in I don't know when," and even the pop charts called its name. Listen to the first few bars of Carla Thomas' "Let Me Be Good to You," or the entirety of Booker T's "Melting Pot," for a scintillating taste of Cropper. During Sam & Dave's recording of "Soul Man," Cropper's fills soared to such an extent that Sam Moore cried out, "Play it, Steve" — and it became part of the money track.

In those days, Cropper played a Fender Telecaster with a rosewood neck, which he felt helped give him "a real nice, biting sound." He worshipped the great Bo Diddley, a man who "literally made his guitar talk," and while Cropper allowed for the fact that some excellent players "change their strings after every solo," he hated new strings. "I change them when they break," he said. "I even rub Chapstick on my strings. It sort of gives you the effect of two or three days of playing them, where you get the grease in there and the dirt." Most crucial, from my point of view, Cropper said he found a sound that "I can almost play a wrong chord and nobody would know the difference. That's how unmelodic it is. It's more percussive."

That was the essence of Steve Cropper, vigorously unconcerned with adulation but striking the chords of salvation. He became a legendary figure in guitarist circles. He evolved into the producer and engineer behind several Stax records and co-wrote several hits, including "Knock On Wood," "In the Midnight Hour" and "(Sittin' On) the Dock of the Bay." The Beatles were in the process of recording their *Sgt. Pepper* album in 1967 when Stax took a star-studded revue to Europe, and when they met Cropper, wrote Guralnick, "They stood in unison and bowed at the waist."

What was it about Stax, exactly? Stewart told Rob Bowman "we could never grab that little thing Motown had. Of course, they couldn't grab ours, either. We envied them being able to cross over to the pop market, but it just wasn't us. We had to do what we knew best."

What they knew, among other things, was how to make a horn chart plunge deep into a listener's soul, there to reside in bliss, always fresh, never duplicated. It was almost exclusively the work of trumpeter Wayne Jackson, who came up with the Mar-Keys ("Last Night"), and saxophonist Andrew Love, who made his name with Willie Mitchell's band ("20-75"). Together, just the two of them, they represented the opposite extreme of intrusive, all-over-the-map horn sections who barge into a song and won't let go. They lingered on single notes, or put a half-dozen together with a feathery touch that amplified, rather than dominated. Anyone could play those charts, but the harmonies are fiercely distinctive and with a common, instantly recognizable thread. I hear the eight-bar horn interlude on "You Don't Know Like I Know" or the rideout to "Just One More Day," to offer just a couple of examples, and I really can't go on. Not before hitting "rewind" and catching it one more time.

Amazingly, Otis Redding was at the heart of all this. I knew there had to be one person behind this sound, such a constant over the years, and I'll be damned if it wasn't one of the greatest *vocalists* of our time. Jackson often told Cropper that recording a Stax session "was like going to church," and it didn't take long for the congregation to assemble. Redding's first Stax record was "These Arms of Mine," in 1962, and as Cropper recalled, "The cat sang about two lines, and everybody just went like this — 'Jesus Christ, this guy's incredible.'"

As he sang, mournfully or in joy, Otis heard accompaniment in his head. As Love recalled, "Otis had a lot to do with the Stax horn sound because he hummed a lot of the lines to us. He'd put the horns in some funny places, too. We'd say, 'Now, wait a minute,' but after you played it through, it was right. It became a certain style." An occasional session sideman, Jim Dickinson, said "Otis would record stripped to the waist. He put bath towels under his arms. He wanted those horn players live on the floor; he'd sing their parts to them and put that whole session together."

As Jackson saw it, "Otis was just born to do that. You can't practice to be that good. He'd run down from his vocal mike down to where the horns were and be shaking his fist at you and singing those parts and it was just electrifying. He'd put that big fist up in the air and strut that stuff at you until you were just foaming at the mouth. We had to calm him down sometimes. But we played exactly what he was singing, and that would be the horn line for the song. We were strictly painting a picture for him to dance in."

The thing about it, as told by saxophonist Floyd Newman, is that "Otis did things in keys like E, A and F-sharp, keys that nobody was playing in. It gave his songs a lot of punch and made you want to pop your fingers. There's not a lot of words on Otis' records, but there are a lot of horn lines. James Brown did the same thing, but Otis' lines were more difficult, rhythmically and harmonically."

Back then, and for years to come, nobody was ever quite the same after hearing James Brown.

He was the funkmeister of all funky funk. "Out of Sight" flat-out changed my life in 1964, making me realize there was a totally original sound out there, and "Papa's Got a Brand New Bag" only amplified the sensation. I remember Otis Redding a bit more fondly, though, in the wake of research. Those musicians' words make it clear that Redding didn't just front his band, he *became* it, with a tender and loving touch. They revered him, and speak to this day of the privilege in recording with him. Brown didn't much care for his guys. They laid down some bad-ass rhythms that had racist grandmothers dancing in Nebraska, but Brown wanted all of the attention lavished upon himself and he'd go weeks without paying them. That's just plain rude. I'm not sure who played drums on "Can't Stand Myself," but I feel like sending him a few bucks right now. Hell, that was nearly fifty years ago and it still seems delivered from the gods.

Everything changed at Stax on December 10, 1967, when Redding, determined to get from Cleveland to a gig in Madison, Wisconsin, died in a plane crash. His twin-engine Beechcraft hurtled into the chilled waters of Lake Monona, also killing several members of the Bar-Kays band. Devastating?

It was as if the label's essence perished right along with him. Redding was just twenty-six years old, and "that took the heart out of Stax," said Stewart. "The day Otis Redding died, that took a lot out of me. I was never the same person. The company was never the same after that."

For me, the post-Otis sound was all about Booker T. and the MG's. They continued to crank out fabulous instrumentals, and I loved seeing John Belushi and Dan Aykroyd enlist Cropper and "Duck" Dunn for the guitar and bass slots in the original Blues Brothers band. Something had to fill that deeper void, though. And I found my resurrection in Tower of Power.

Less than six months after Redding's plane went down, Emilio "Mimi" Castillo met Doc Kupka and formed the Oakland-based band. As I began my fifth year at Cal in 1970 (one did quite a bit of stalling to stay out of Vietnam), Tower's first album came out. Here was the next step in R&B, and as tradition dictated, it was a titanic leap forward. I have a single, shining memory of that final year, spent in a studio apartment on Durant Avenue, and that's listening to *East Bay Grease,* over and over. Blown away by "Back on the Streets Again," charmed by "Sparkling in the Sand," knocked clean out by Dave Garibaldi's drumming, Mimi's soulful vocals and some spectacularly clever horn charts, I became a fan for life. These guys were onto something entirely new. Just like Ray Charles, Smokey Robinson, Otis Redding and James Brown, their stuff sounds just as fresh today, as invigorating as the sunrise.

The Tower of Power horns at their finest:
Greg Adams, Mic Gilette, Steve Kupka,
Lenny Pickett and Mimi Castillo.

Chapter 8

On the Retro Highway

Most of us listen to music in a casual way. It sets a party mood, frames a workplace, serves as background. I can't do it that way. I'm my father's son in that regard. He'd gather friends — musicians, cosmopolitan types, anyone who got it — and bring them into his work studio with cocktails in hand. There he would unleash Mahalia Jackson, Renata Tebaldi, Harry James, Stravinsky, even his own stuff (say, Sinatra or *Manhattan Tower*) through his professional-quality equipment and JBL speakers. No one would make a sound, save a burst of appreciative laughter or an unbridled reaction ("Unh") to something especially pure. With the control room close at hand, Gor listened from a standing position, hands in his pockets, head tilted slightly down. When the piece was finished, exuberant conversation began. They'd all been there, lived that experience many times before. And then all would go quiet for what followed.

I wouldn't be in that room. Heavens no, not at age eight or twelve or even eighteen. It was just so *heavy*. I'd be playing ball or gliding across waves in the ocean, and come nightfall, I had my own little musical haven inside the main house. It would be a very good night if the Impressions, Jackie Ross or Junior Walker lit up the KGFJ airwaves, or perhaps a taste of the early Rolling Stones (ardent followers of American R&B) on the conventional rock stations. I was always alone, an only child reveling in the solitude.

I've got a pretty fair audio setup in my current home, but the music rarely comes on. I'm far too busy trying to stay current with the sports world. The car is my sanctuary. I turn the ignition, activate the CD player and ease into my separate life. I'm a completely different person than anyone has ever seen. Free of inhibition, with nothing going on but the highway, I croon the harmonies and play steering-wheel drums and slap my thigh. How I'd love to spring that person loose in public, but the embarrassment … I wouldn't dare. Not unless I looked like Terrence Howard, sang like Sam Cooke and danced like Gregory Hines.

I realize I'm hardly alone in this sing-in-the-shower groove. I pass by kindred souls just rockin' out like mad. I wish things could be exactly the same with someone in the passenger seat, but no — add just one person, and I'm as stoic as the Lincoln Memorial. Because then you're listening through someone else: my daughter, with her very contemporary interests, or my wife, whose retro heart leans more toward Elton John and Van Morrison.

I never used to care much about lyrics. I judged records entirely on the rhythms, vocal phrasings and musicianship, and they could have been singing about the potted plants of southern Norway, for all I cared. That changed in my college days, thanks to Dylan, Joni Mitchell, the Sons of Champlin ("*In a world where all of us are radical, now is not the time for a sabbatical*") and so many others. Now, though, I'm on a Motown/soul music discovery mission. I'm getting totally into the words. Although I didn't quite grasp the significance at the time, these were *love* songs, unveiled with tenderness and compassion.

There's a girl and a guy, and oh lord, such foolish pride. Innocence isn't quite the mood, not when it's coming from Wilson Pickett or Tina Turner. But listeners instantly related to the joy and heartache of serious relationships. You can almost hear them: "How Sweet It Is? Since I Lost My Baby? You're tellin' my story right there."

I guess I didn't take much notice back then because elite recordings always had killer lyrics, way back through the decades, and my father was right up front. But things changed over the years. Oh my *god*, such a change. The onset of rap music brought to my mind two horrific developments: repetitive instrumentation, showing no real creativity or imagination, and downright nasty words.

Believe me, I get it. The mainstays of rap music target a deeply jaded generation, and it really isn't like listening to music at all. It's being *spoken* to. This is how it IS, and I'm a little bit PISSED right now, and somebody's got to PAY, and it just might be your MOTHER if it comes to that.

Call me an incurable romantic, but I don't need the lecture. I ask music to soothe my mind, teach me something; I don't mix cold-blooded murder with my respite. I savor the elements of class and restraint.

In the Temptations' "The Girl's All Right With Me," here's Eddie Kendricks at your service:

When I visit at her home
Other fellas never ring her phone
She lets them know just where they stand
She tells them all that I'm her man
And when we're out on a date
Other fellas wait 'til I walk away
They try to beat my time
She tells 'em in a nice way she's mine all mine

In a *nice* way? The other fellas didn't beat the crap out of Eddie? How lovely.

I could call up dastardly rap lyrics all day long, but here's a sample from Mickey Avalon's "My Dick," and I'm not kidding: *My dick — don't fit down the chimney/ Yo' dick — like kid from the Philippines. …*

Wait, let me correct myself; I *couldn't* call up rap lyrics all day long. I don't even let 'em in the door. I hear about eighteen seconds of anything and I'm gone. Clever, bold, truth be told — I get all that. These cats assemble spoken rhymes like nobody's business. It's just that I'll take a pass. I'll call up the Drifters and make things right.

See, I figure stress takes years off your life.
Perhaps that's a fallacy, but I've always believed it.
I long ago vowed that two things wouldn't kill me:
second-hand smoke and anxiety. Just won't happen.
All other ghastly possibilities remain in play.

Meanwhile, here are a few other discoveries I've made of late, delving into the Motown lyrics and finding precious gems:

Smokey Robinson and the Miracles:
Every time you need some affection
The one you love goes in another direction
You just sit there in a daze, reminiscin'
When you know some other lips she's been kissin'

The Temptations:
To get fire from a match
You got to strike it
To get the feeling from a kiss
You got to like it
To get ashes from wood
You got to burn it
And if you want my love
You got to earn it

The Supremes:
How can Mary tell me what to do
When she lost her love so true?
And Flo, she don't know
'Cause the boy she loves is a Romeo

Sam Hawkins:
She'll put her cigarette out
And give me that little smile
She'll put a stack of records on
Ain't be a slow one in the pile

In the coming months, I'd imagine the focus will change. I'll listen strictly for Benjamin's drum riffs, the fabulously crisp guitar, the never-intrusive piano, the wildly inventive forms of alternate percussion. Always, motoring down the road with a satisfied soul, I'll find myself profoundly removed from that little hair salon in '65. At the same time, there's a deep and unmistakable connection. Back then, I was an impressionable kid wanting desperately to be old. I'm now in my mid-sixties, hearing the music that shaped my life, and feeling younger by the minute. I kind of like that deal.

A not-so-sober moment with Tower's Steve Kupka,
Marin County, early 1980s.

A GATHERING OF LISTS

Songs That Changed an Awful Lot

I Got a Woman: Ray Charles, 1955

Change Gonna Come: Sam Cooke

We're a Winner: Impressions

Shotgun/Road Runner: Junior Walker

Green Onions: Booker T. and the MG's

Out of Sight: James Brown

These Arms of Mine: Otis Redding

Fingertips Part II: Stevie Wonder, age 12

(Say It Loud) I'm Black and I'm Proud: James Brown

Back on the Streets Again: Tower of Power

10 Songs That Defined Motown

Can I Get a Witness: Marvin Gaye

The Tracks of My Tears: Miracles

Where Did Our Love Go: Supremes

My Girl: Temptations

Baby I Need Your Lovin': Four Tops

My Guy: Mary Wells

Uptight: Stevie Wonder

Nowhere to Run: Martha and the Vandellas

Please Mr. Postman: Marvelettes

Do You Love Me: The Contours

Great Female Vocals

A Fool in Love: Tina Turner

Do I Love You: Ronnie Bennett/The Ronettes

Helpless: Kim Weston

Every Little Bit Hurts: Brenda Holloway

You Turned My Bitter Into Sweet: Mary Love

Think: Lyn Collins

You Beat Me to the Punch: Mary Wells

Mama Said: Shirley Alston Reeves/The Shirelles

Cleanup Woman: Betty Wright

Don't Lose Control of Your Soul: Linda Tillery/
    Loading Zone

I Just Want to Make Love to You: Lydia Pense/
    Cold Blood
Drown in My Own Tears: Aretha Franklin, and her
    church-inspired piano

A Thousand Crushes: Girl Groups

Got to Have Your Love: The Sapphires
Best Part of Breakin' Up: The Ronettes
Sally Go Round the Roses: The Jaynetts
Good Night Baby: The Butterflys
Will You Still Love Me Tomorrow: The Shirelles
Too Many Fish in the Sea: The Marvelettes
He Was Really Sayin' Somethin': The Velvelettes
Watch What Happens: The Royalettes
The 81: Candy and the Kisses
Mister Lee: The Bobbettes
Tell Him: The Exciters
Good Time Tonight: The Soul Sisters

Vintage Motown Openings (instantly hooked)

You're a Wonderful One: Marvin Gaye

The Way You Do the Things You Do: Temptations

Shotgun: Junior Walker

Needle in a Haystack: Velvelettes

The Girl's All Right With Me: Temptations

Shake Me, Wake Me: Four Tops

Baby Don't You Do it: Marvin Gaye

Come See About Me: Supremes

Ain't That Peculiar: Marvin Gaye

Ain't Too Proud to Beg: Temptations

The Most Soulful Humming

Tina Turner, at the end of "I Don't Need Nobody
    Like You"

Edwin Starr, in the bridge of "Agent Double-O Soul"

Major Lance, throughout Um, Um-Um-Um-Um, Um

The Stax Horns at Their Finest

Let Me Be Good To You: Carla Thomas

You Don't Know Like I Know: Sam and Dave

Hold On I'm Comin': Sam and Dave

Fa-Fa-Fa-Fa-Fa (Sad Song): Otis Redding

Don't Mess With Cupid: Otis Redding

Just One More Day: Otis Redding

Otis Redding Favorites

Pain in My Heart

Nobody's Fault but Mine

Amen

My Lover's Prayer

Try a Little Tenderness

I've Been Loving You Too Long

Old Man Trouble

Best Use of the Spoken Word

Lou Rawls at the beginning of "Dead End Street"

Memorable Duets

Once Upon a Time: Marvin Gaye and Mary Wells

You're Gonna Mess Up a Good Thing: Fontella Bass and Bobby McClure

Let It Be Me: Jerry Butler and Betty Everett

Ain't No Mountain High Enough: Marvin Gaye and Tammi Terrell

You've Got What It Takes: Dinah Washington and Brook Benton

You're Gonna Miss Me: Bass & McClure

That Old Black Magic: Louis Prima and Keely Smith

Sixteen A-Listers

It's All Over Now: The Valentinos

The Entertainer: Tony Clarke

Follow Your Heart: The Manhattans

Ain't Nobody Home: Howard Tate

Heart Full of Love: The Invincibles

Leavin' Here: Eddie Holland

Come Back Baby: Roddie Joy

Showtime: The Detroit Emeralds

Love's Gonna Do You In: The Autographs

I'll Love You Forever: The Holidays

I'm So Proud: Impressions

Tramp: Lowell Fulsom

Somebody's Cuttin' On My Groove: Wayne Cochran
Nothing Can Stop Me: Gene Chandler
Never Like this Before: William Bell
The Woman's Got Soul: Impressions

Great Male Vocals
Ask the Lonely: Levi Stubbs/Four Tops
Up on the Roof: Rudy Lewis/The Drifters
Pride and Joy: Marvin Gaye
There Ain't Nothin' You Can Do: Bobby Bland
I'll Try Something New: Smokey Robinson/
    The Miracles
Lonely Teardrops: Jackie Wilson
Chain Gang: Sam Cooke
Hitch Hike: Marvin Gaye
This Can't Be True: Eddie Holman
It's You That I Need: David Ruffin
Hold On Baby: Sam Hawkins
Love's Gone Bad: Chris Clark
You're Still a Young Man: Rick Stevens/Tower of Power
Can't Hide Love: Maurice White/Earth, Wind & Fire
Find Yourself Another Girl: Jerry Butler
Ebb Tide: Bobby Hatfield/Righteous Brothers
Buzz Buzz Buzz: Huey Lewis/& the News
It's Not the Crime: Emilio Castillo/Tower of Power

Best Use of the Final Seconds for Choice Lyrics

That's the Way Love Is: Bobby Bland

The Best James Brown Grooves

Papa's Got a Brand New Bag

Mother Popcorn, into Give It Up or Turn It Loose
(on the "Sex Machine" live album)

I Feel Good '75 (Hard to find, but worth it)

Can't Stand Myself

Papa Don't Take No Mess

The Payback

Lickin' Stick

A Dozen Fine Instrumentals

Gonzo: James Booker

The Kicker: Bill Doggett

20-75: Willie Mitchell

Oakland Stroke: Tower of Power

Valdez in the Country: Cold Blood

Twine Time: Alvin Cash and the Crawlers

Squib Cakes: Tower of Power

The Cat: Jimmy Smith

Hole in the Wall: The Packers

Mahdi (The Expected One) Tower of Power

Melting Pot: Booker T. and the MG's

Watermelon Man: Mongo Santamaria

Best Tower of Power Grooves

Skatin' On Thin Ice

What Is Hip

You Strike My Main Nerve

Oakland Stroke (killer visual on youtube:
    Call up "Rocco Prestia of Tower of Power:
    Oakland Stroke," from Bass Day '98)

Stroke '75

On the Serious Side

Get Yo' Feet Back on the Ground

Soul Vaccination

Knock Yourself Out (rhythm section, about 4:40 in)

Sparkling in the Sand (jazzy interlude)

Favorite Drummers

David Garibaldi

Steve Gadd

Sandy McKee

Bobby Colomby

Danny Saraphine

Harvey Mason

Grady Tate

Bill (Plumpy) Bowen

Benny Benjamin

Clyde Stubblefield

Mitch Mitchell

Miles Teller (in "Whiplash" — nice job)

Cool It, Dad's Home

Desafinado: Stan Getz, from The Bossa Nova Years album

Oh, By Jingo!: Billy May, from Sorta Dixie

I Got It: Jimmie Lunceford

Potato Head Blues: Louis Armstrong

Arabian Dance, from the Nutcracker

Nice Work If You Can Get It: Ella Fitzgerald

Hi-Fly: Lambert, Hendricks & Ross

Can't See For Lookin': The Nat Cole Trio

India: Erroll Garner

2nd Symphony: Sibelius

Sinatra's Favorite Vocals With the Jenkins Orchestra

It Was a Very Good Year

This Is All I Ask

Laura

Lonely Town

Send in the Clowns

But I Loved Her

The Future

(These I know for certain)

Gor's Favorite Work Outside of Sinatra

Working with arranger Victor Young and an all-star ensemble, including Red Ballard and Jack Jenney, with the Isham Jones Band, 1930s

Writing with Benny Goodman, 1934, the genesis of "Goodbye"

Working with Dick Haymes, Martha Tilton, Pauline Byrne, the Nat Cole Trio and other greats of L.A. radio national broadcasts, 1940s

Recording "Blueberry Hill" and other cuts with Louis Armstrong, 1949

Defying anti-Communist paranoia and recording the Weavers, 1950

Recording "February Fever" and other Jenkins
originals on the *Almanac* album, 1955
Conducting Judy Garland at the Old Dominion
Theater, London, 1957
Recording "Stardust" and "Paradise" with Nat Cole
Any session with Eddie Miller, Matty Matlock and
Nick Fatool, the kings of Dixieland
Writing and conducting concept albums *Manhattan
Tower* and *Seven Dreams*
Recording the album *Soul of a People,* his all-
instrumental arrangements of traditional Jewish
melodies, 1968 (knockout cut: "My Yiddishe
Mama")
Recording *A Little Touch of Schmilsson in the Night*
with Harry Nilsson in London, 1973

Some of Mom's Favorite Vocalists

Sonny Boy Williamson
Chippie Hill
Cousin Joe
Bessie Smith
Mildred Bailey
Charlie LaVere
Jack Jones
Andy Williams

Aretha Franklin

Ray Charles

(Beverly from a long-ago radio interview: "I went down to New Orleans one time and heard a blues singer called Cousin Joe. He was wonderful, had one of my favorite blues lines of all time. Talkin' about his girl: 'She come in, had a fifty-dollar hat on a nickel head.'")

Music for Driving Through the San Francisco Fog

Guinnevere: Crosby, Stills & Nash

She Has Funny Cars: Jefferson Airplane

Up From the Skies: Jimi Hendrix

Small World: Huey Lewis & The News, Stan Getz,
    Tower of Power horn section

Latin Hags: Terry Haggerty

Wicked Game: Chris Isaak (instrumental version)

Samba Pa Ti: Santana

Amnesia: The Tubes

Misery Isn't Free: Sons of Champlin

Another Country: Electric Flag

The Sophisticates Stop By

Witchcraft: Frank Sinatra

Beyond the Sea: Bobby Darin

I Wanna Be Around: Tony Bennett

Route 66 Theme: Nelson Riddle

That's My Kick: Errol Garner

The Seventh Son: Mose Allison

Soul Sauce: Cal Tjader

How Insensitive: Wes Montgomery

My Sweetness: Stuff

You've Changed: Dexter Gordon

The Telephone Song: Stan Getz and Astrud Gilberto

I'll Close My Eyes: Jimmy Smith and Kenny Burrell

Take Twenty: Mainstream DJ For a Night

Deacon Blues: Steely Dan

Bean Time: Leo Kottke

So Begins the Task: Stephen Stills/Manassas

Mud Slide Slim: James Taylor

Midnight Rider: Allman Brothers

Night in the City: Joni Mitchell

Oxford Town: Bob Dylan

All Over: Phoebe Snow

Teen Town: Weather Report

This Must Be the Place: Talking Heads

Smile Please: Stevie Wonder

Time Will Bring You Love: Bill Champlin

New Frontier: Donald Fagen

Bang Bang: The Joe Cuba Sextet

At the Party: Hector Rivera

You Know What I Mean: Jeff Beck

2120 South Michigan Avenue: Rolling Stones

Nice Feelin': Rita Coolidge

Lost in the Love of You: Livingston Taylor

Riviera Paradise: Stevie Ray Vaughan

The Ultimate Lyrics Contrast

About as much as one can take from

    Bobby Goldsboro's "Watching Scotty Grow":

There he sits with a pen and yellow pad

What a handsome lad

That's my boy

You can have your TV and your night clubs

And you can have your drive-in picture show

I'll stay here with my little man near

We'll listen to the radio

Biding my time, and watching Scotty grow

Riding on daddy's shoulder off to bed

Old sleepy head

That's my boy

Got to have a drink of water and a story read

A teddy bear named Fred

That's my boy

And to get down deepest, some Koko Taylor:

Tell automatic Slim

To tell razor-totin' Jim

Tell butcher knife-totin' Nanny

To tell fast-talkin' Fanny

We gonna pitch a ball

Down to the union hall

We gonna romp and tromp 'til midnight
We gonna fuss and fight 'til daylight

Tell Fats and washbone Sam
That everybody gonna jam
Tell shakin' boxcar Joe
We got sawdust on the floor
And when the fish scent fill the air
There'll be snuff juice everywhere

Tell cooda-crawlin' Red
To tell abyssinia Ned
Tell old Pistol Pete
To tell everybody he meet
Tonight we need no rest
We gonna really throw a mess
We gonna knock down all the windows
Gonna kick down all the doors
We gonna pitch a Wang Dang Doodle
All night long
—*"Wang Dang Doodle"*

About
the Series

This memoir of Bruce Jenkins' love of music is the second in Wellstone Books' "Music That Changed My Life" series, featuring small volumes with attention-grabbing cover illustrations by Mark Ulriksen that we hope will prompt you to lean into your love of music. They're quick reads, full of honest emotion, best read with music playing in the background. Wellstone Books publishes personal writing that is not afraid to inspire, and what inspires more than a deep connection to music?

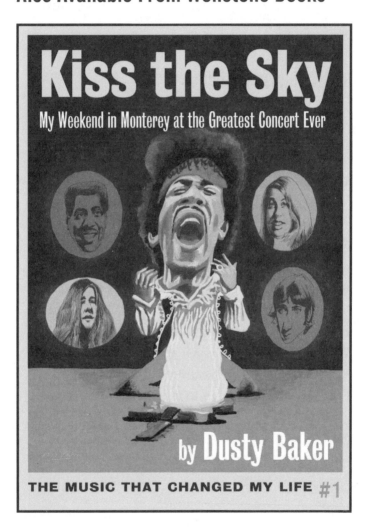

For his eighteenth birthday, Dusty Baker's mother gave him a great present: Two tickets to the Monterey Pop Festival of June 1967, a three-day event featuring more than thirty bands, and use of the family station wagon for the weekend so young Dusty could drive down from Sacramento to the Monterey Bay. He was another young person, trying to take it all in, sleeping on the beach with his buddy, having the time of his life soaking up the vibe and every different musical style represented there. Baker's lifelong love of music was set in motion, his wide-ranging, eclectic tastes, everything from country to hip-hop. He also caught the Jimi Hendrix Experience, who put on such a show that to this day Baker calls Hendrix the most exciting performer he's ever seen. He went on to years of friendship with musicians from B.B. King and John Lee Hooker to Elvin Bishop. This account grabs a reader from page one and never lets up.

"At its best, the book evokes not only the pleasure of music, but the connection between that experience and the joy of sports," NewYorker.com writes.

#1 in Wellstone Books' "Music That Changed My Life" series.

WELLSTONE CENTER
IN THE REDWOODS

The Wellstone Center in the Redwoods, a writer's
retreat center in Northern California, publishes
books under its Wellstone Books imprint and offers
weeklong writing residencies, monthlong writing
fellowships and weekend writing workshops; we
also host regular Author Talk events. Founded
by Sarah Ringler and Steve Kettmann, WCR has
been hailed in the *San Jose Mercury News* as a
beautiful, inspiring environment that is "kind of
like heaven" for writers and in the *San Francisco
Chronicle* as a place "where inspiration seems to
just hang in the air," and featured in *San Francisco
Magazine*'s "Best of the Bay" issue. Visit our website at www.wellstoneredwoods.org and email us at
info@wellstoneredwoods.org